CHEESE

FROM FONDUE TO CHEESECAKE

CHEESE

FROM FONDUE TO CHEESECAKE

Contributing Editor
Fiona Beckett

RYLAND
PETERS
& SMALL

LONDON NEW YORK

DESIGNER Pamela Daniels
EDITOR Sharon Cochrane
PRODUCTION Sheila Smith
PICTURE RESEARCH Emily Westlake
ART DIRECTOR Gabriella Le Grazie
PUBLISHING DIRECTOR Alison Starling

First published in the United States in 2005
by Ryland Peters & Small, Inc.
519 Broadway, 5th Floor
New York, NY 10012
www.rylandpeters.com

10 9 8 7 6 5 4 3 2 1

Library of Congress Cataloging-in-Publication Data

Cheese : from fondue to cheesecake /
contributing editor Fiona Beckett.
    p. cm.
  Includes index.
  ISBN 1-84172-810-1
  1. Cookery (Cheese) I. Beckett, Fiona.
  TX759.5.C48C365 2005
  641.6'73--dc22
                        2004019114

Some of Fiona Beckett's text was first published
in *Cheese: Discovering, Exploring, Enjoying* (also
published by Ryland Peters & Small). For recipe
credits please see page 144.

NOTE Unpasteurized cheese and uncooked or
partly cooked eggs should not be served to the very
young, the very old, those with compromised
immune systems, or to pregnant women.

Printed in China.

CONTENTS

INTRODUCTION

Few foods can match cheese for variety and sheer unadulterated pleasure. The tangy freshness of a day-old goat cheese, bought straight from the farmers' market. The satisfying bite of a carefully matured, mellow Cheddar. A gently oozing Brie, just begging to be partnered by a hunk of crusty baguette. Drifts of freshly grated Parmesan settling on top of your favorite pasta sauce. The crisp topping on a baked macaroni and cheese, to be saved for the final mouthful. Cheese surely rivals chocolate as the most difficult food to resist.

At its best, it is one of the finest handmade products, produced by passionate individuals who supervise the whole process from start to finish—rearing their own animals and carefully bringing their cheeses to perfection in cool cellars and maturing rooms. Even the poorest gentleman farmer can make great cheese—it's at the same time one of the most simple and sophisticated of foods. Yet all too often we treat it without enough respect, eating it straight from the refrigerator, keeping it too long, never giving ourselves a chance to enjoy its full flavor and richness.

Well, here's a chance to put that right. *Cheese: from Fondue to Cheesecake* is the one book you need to enjoy cheese to the maximum, introducing you to the extraordinary variety and versatility of this amazing food. Find out about the many different styles of cheese and what affects their flavor and texture. Learn how to pick a good cheese and how to

ensure it remains at its best. Discover what makes
a perfect cheeseboard or how to serve cheese more
simply and originally with just one or two well-chosen
accompaniments, including great home-baked bread.

Through the sumptuously illustrated recipes, you will see
just how versatile cheese can be and how you can use it
in the simplest and most celebratory of meals. You can
crumble it, slice it, or grate it. Broil, bake, or sauté it. You
can serve it cold (or, rather, at room temperature), warm,
or hot. As a salad or as a light-as-air stuffing with fresh
herbs or greens. As an elegant terrine or a flaky phyllo
turnover. You can feast on fondue and on fabulous pastas,
pizzas, and risottos. You can find it in the most tempting
desserts—from ice creams to irresistible cheesecakes.

Through each recipe you'll find the flavors and ingredients
that complement particular styles of cheese—how Belgian
endive and walnuts set off Roquefort, for example. Blissful
marriages like tomatoes and mozzarella, red bell peppers
and goat cheese, feta and mint, pecorino and pears, and
strawberries and mascarpone will inspire you to experiment
and create exciting combinations of your own.

Above all, the recipes in this book are made to share with
family and friends—appealing to vegetarians and non-
vegetarians alike—and will introduce them to the pleasure
of a lifetime's love of cheese.

CHEESE BASICS

If you want to get the maximum enjoyment out of cheese, it pays to know a bit about it. What affects the taste of different cheeses and how to skillfully combine them on a cheeseboard. Where to go and what to look for when you buy them. How to store and serve them so that you can be confident of showing them at their best. Some simple ideas for pairing cheeses with fruits and other complementary ingredients such as nuts and olives. And last, but not least, a guide to the best wines to partner with different types of cheese.

SOFT AND SEMI-SOFT CHEESES

From deliciously fresh goat cheeses to the rich creamy indulgence of gooey cheeses like Vacherin, soft and semi-soft cheeses are some of the most enjoyable to eat—the perfect way to start exploring the cheese world.

VERY YOUNG CHEESES

Cheeses that are days—or hours—rather than weeks old are deliciously light and moussey, the curds just separated from the whey. Goat's and sheep's milk cheeses are often made in this style, and can be rolled in ash or fresh herbs for serving. Also sold young are fresh, milky mozzarella and its by-product, ricotta, which is made from the left-over whey. This style of cheese can be kept for a longer period of time if preserved in brine or oil, like feta and haloumi.

GOAT CHEESE

The flavor of goat cheese evolves more rapidly than many other cheeses, so that by the time it is ten days old, the taste may be quite pronounced. Over a few weeks it will develop a natural rind and harden so that the flavor becomes piquant and nutty. Goat's milk cheeses are produced in a variety of shapes, from small buttons like Crottin de Chavignol to logs and pyramids, or they may be wrapped in vine or chestnut leaves like the Provençal cheese Banon.

SARIETTE DE BANON

BRILLAT-SAVARIN

BRIE DE MEAUX

TALEGGIO

EPOISSES

SOFT WHITE RIND CHEESES

Brie and Camembert are the two best known examples of this style of cheese which—when young at least—has a delicate mushroomy flavor, creamy texture, and a soft, downy, pure white rind. Most are made from cow's milk. With age, they develop in flavor, the center becoming softer and richer until it oozes out of the rind (though this is frowned upon by expert *affineurs*). Plenty of artisan producers outside France make cheeses in this style including Doeling Camembert from Arkansas and Old Chatham's Hudson Valley Camembert from New York. Other examples include Chaource and the heart-shaped Coeur de Neufchâtel from France and Cooleeney from Ireland.

VERY CREAMY CHEESES

These are made in a similar style to soft rind cheeses, but with the addition of cream, which gives them a buttery, unctuous, almost dessert-like richness. They include French cheeses such as Brillat-Savarin, Boursault, and Explorateur.

SEMI-SOFT CHEESES (MEDIUM-MATURED)

A description that covers a multitude of unpressed cheeses that share a supple springy consistency and a soft pliable, sometimes sticky rind. Many are known as "washed rind." This means the cheese has been washed or rubbed in brine, wine, or cider, giving the cheese a rich fruity flavor and the rind a deep orange color. France has been the master of this style of cheese since the days it was made in monasteries; in fact it's often referred to as Trappist cheese. Young—or commercially produced—washed rind cheeses such as Saint-Nectaire, Reblochon, and Pont L'Evêque are comparatively mild. But, along with others like Livarot and Maroilles, they can develop pungent flavors and strong, barnyardy aromas. There are some fine Irish examples such as Ardrahan, Gubbeen, and Milleens that are milder. Taleggio is a great Italian version. Good starting points for exploring this style are the less assertive Chaumes, Morbier, and Port Salut from France, Danish Havarti, and German Tilsiter.

GOUDA-STYLE CHEESES

You could argue about how best to describe waxy cheeses like Gouda. Technically they're classified semi-soft, though aged Gouda has all the firmness, bite, and richness of flavor of a hard cheese. However, if it comes from a supermarket, it's more than likely to be mild to mellow and more soft than hard. Other examples would be Edam, Colby, and young British and Irish Gouda-style cheeses such as Coolea and Teifi.

VACHERIN

So special is Vacherin that France and Switzerland, which both border the area where it's made, have long battled over the name. The more widely available French version is technically referred to as Mont d'Or, though most shops simply describe it as Vacherin. Made from unpasteurized milk from cows that graze in the Jura mountains, it has a fabulous rich, mellow taste and velvety texture. Only available from September to March, it is presented in a lidded wooden box and when fully ripe, you can spoon it out.

HARD CHEESES

The word "hard" applies to cheeses with a firm texture which have been pressed or subjected to heat. They are generally aged and have a hard, inedible rind, though some like Caerphilly or Lancashire can be mild and crumbly.

WENSLEYDALE

TRADITIONAL REGIONAL CHEESES

There is a range of historic "territorial cheeses" from different parts of England, the recipes of which can date back as far as the eleventh century. Some are mild, creamy, and crumbly like Caerphilly, Wensleydale, and Cheshire (which was mentioned in the Domesday book of 1056). Lancashire can have more bite, while Red Leicester and Double Gloucester, which owe their orange color to the natural coloring annatto, are richer and nuttier. It's always worth seeking out matured farmhouse versions of these cheeses since mass-produced ones can be bland.

HARD SHEEP'S CHEESE

Often the product of inhospitable pastures and subsistence farming, sheep's milk cheeses provided vital sustenance for poorer communities across southern Europe and were made to last through the winter. Today, such cheeses as pecorino from Italy (and its regional variations pecorino Romano, pecorino Sardo, and pecorino Toscano), Spanish Manchego, Roncal, and Zamorano, and Etorki and Ossau-Iraty-Brébis from the French side of the Pyrenees are highly regarded for their complexity and depth of flavor. A new generation of cheesemakers in the United Kingdom and the United States has also chosen to work with sheep's milk rather than cow's milk, creating modern classics such as Berkswell, Spenwood, and Vermont Shepherd. When young, this style of cheese has a subtle salty, nutty tang.

CHEDDAR

This is the most popular style of cheese in the world, though true Cheddar is only made in the counties of Somerset, Dorset, and Devon in the southwest of England. The flavor can range from mild and mellow to nutty and piquant depending upon whether it is commercially made or aged for many months by a farmhouse producer. Cheddar is aged for an average of about four months, although artisanal specimens can be aged for as long as 24 months, sometimes longer. The cheeses are made in huge dramatic looking "truckles" weighing 52 pounds or more and are traditionally wrapped in cheesecloth and sealed with wax. Almost all Cheddars and Cheddar-style cheeses are made with cow's milk. Highly regarded English producers include Montgomery and Keen's. Scotland, Australia, Canada, and New Zealand also have a long history of making good-quality Cheddar-style cheeses and there are some good artisanal examples in the US such as Grafton Village Cheddar. If you like Cheddar, you will also like a similar cheese from France called Cantal.

SWISS-STYLE

Although thought of as Swiss, cheeses such as Gruyère and Emmental are also made in France; they share the same firm, smooth, close texture which derives from heating the curds then pressing them heavily. The distinctive holes in Emmental and similar cheeses come from bubbles of gas that develop during the fermentation process. The taste is fresh and aromatic, becoming nuttier with age. They also melt well, so are often used in cooking. Traditionally they are made from unpasteurized cow's milk from Alpine herds. Less well-known cheeses that are made in a similar way include Beaufort and Comté from the French side of the Alps, Swiss Appenzeller and Tête de Moine, and Norwegian Jarlsberg. Newer cheeses made in this style include Gabriel from Ireland, Roth Käse Gruyere from the US, and Heidi Gruyere from Tasmania.

PROVOLONE

Scalded and then molded into a myriad of different shapes, this buttercup yellow *pasta filata* (stretched curd) cheese is a staple of Italian delis. It can be mild (*dolce*) or aged for up to two years (*piccante*).

DUTCH-STYLE

While much of the Gouda you find is quite soft in texture, mature Gouda is a hard, slightly granular cheese with a rich, nutty flavor much admired by other cheesemakers who have copied it all over the world. Examples are Coolea from West Cork in Ireland, Welsh Teifi, Mahoe Aged Gouda and Meyer Vintage Gouda from New Zealand, and Californian Bulk Farm Gouda. Deep orange French Mimolette, made just over the border from Holland, is one of the best cheeses to serve with red Bordeaux.

GRATING CHEESES

The king of grating cheeses is undoubtedly Parmesan. This term tends to be used for any cheese made in a similar crystalline, crumbly style, but true Parmesan is labeled Parmigiano-Reggiano and is made in the Emilia-Romagna region of Italy. It is usually aged for one to two years, but can be aged for up to four. Grana Padano, which looks very similar, is usually younger and can come from anywhere in Italy. Other good grating cheeses include pecorino Romano (see opposite), Swiss Sbrinz, and Vella dry jack from California.

PARMIGIANO-REGGIANO

BERKSWELL

MONTGOMERY'S CHEDDAR

KEEN'S CHEDDAR

PECORINO

CABRALES

FOURME D'AMBERT

BLUE CHEESES

A colorful addition to any cheeseboard, blue cheeses are distinctive in their appeal. Harmless molds introduced into the cheese allow the characteristic greenish-blue "veins" to develop.

MILD CREAMY BLUES

Soft, white rinded, Brie-style cheeses can be made in a blue version—such as Bresse Bleu and Cambozola, a modern cross between Camembert and Gorgonzola. Mild (*dolce*) Gorgonzola (see opposite) or dolcelatte, as it is sometimes known, also falls into this category—a good starting point for those new to blue.

STRONG, TANGY BLUES

These are blues with real bite. Roquefort (see opposite) is the best known, but other sheep's milk cheeses such as Beenleigh Blue from Devon, Scottish Lanark Blue, and Spanish Cabrales and Valdeon pack a similar punch.

MATURE, MELLOW BLUES

Mature blues combine a sharp, assertive flavor with a rich, creamy texture which comes from several weeks' maturing. Most are made from pasteurized or unpasteurized cow's milk and have a rough, crumbly grayish or orangey crust. They include top English and Irish blues such as Stilton (see opposite), Blue Vinny, Shropshire Blue, and Cashel Blue, as well as French blues such as Bleu d'Auvergne, Bleu de Gex, and Fourme d'Ambert— a fine traditional cheese from the mountainous Auvergne region. Other examples include America's Jersey Blue and Great Hill Blue, and Australia's award-winning Gippsland Blue.

STILTON

GORGONZOLA

ROQUEFORT

The world's best blues

STILTON

Arguably the greatest English cheese, production of which is only allowed in a very limited area of Derbyshire, Leicestershire, and Nottinghamshire, in the heartland of the country. Made from cow's milk and characterized by its creamy texture, mature mellow flavor, and distinctive rough, crumbly grayish rind, it's the traditional cheese to serve at Christmas. Colston Bassett is the most famous producer.

GORGONZOLA

Rich, lush Gorgonzola, made using cow's milk, comes from Lombardy and Piedmont in the northwest of Italy. It can be comparatively mild (*dolce*) or strong (*naturale* or *piccante*) and is always sold wrapped in foil which helps preserve its creamy texture. Gorgonzola also lends itself well to cooking, adding a creaminess and richness of flavor to dishes such as risotto (see page 74) and fondue (see page 88).

ROQUEFORT

The strongest and saltiest of blue cheeses, Roquefort is the espresso coffee of the cheese world—a real artisanal unpasteurized sheep's cheese that requires time to fully appreciate. Roquefort is still made in caves in Combalou in the southwest of France where it has been produced since Roman times. The French venerate it like foie gras and truffles, often serving it with the fine dessert wine, Sauternes.

STRONG CHEESES

Not everyone likes strong, pungent

cheeses but aficionados adore them.

STRONG FRENCH CHEESES

Although the word "strong" covers a range of styles, the majority come from the semi-soft, washed rind style, the classic French "smelly cheese." If kept in perfect condition they can be magnificent, but they should be put on a cheeseboard with caution as they can make wine matching tricky. You can find milder versions of these cheeses, but if you spot the following on a cheese counter or trolley, expect them to pack quite a punch: Ami du Chambertin, Epoisses, Livarot, Maroilles, and Munster from France, and Limburger from Germany.

UNUSUAL FLAVORS

Expect the unexpected. Cheeses that don't taste like any others you've tasted before include the deep caramel-colored, almost sweet Gjetost, a hugely popular cheese from Norway, and Hungarian Liptauer, an intensely spicy soft cheese seasoned with garlic, capers, anchovies, and paprika.

POWERFUL BLUES

Strong and salty cheeses such as Roquefort and Spanish Cabrales can overwhelm other cheeses on a cheeseboard, so use them with care.

FLAVORED CHEESES

Cheese can be flavored with any number of ingredients from apricots to Worcestershire sauce and chutney. Most tend to be made by large commercial companies, though herbs, garlic, and spices are all used by artisanal producers either to flavor the cheese or to replace the rind. The most successful are:

• **Herbs**. Popular—along with garlic—in soft French cheeses such as Boursin and Le Roulé and for flavoring the exterior of goat's milk cheeses such as Chèvrefeuille and the Corsican Fleur du Maquis. They are also used in some traditional English hard cheeses such as Sage Derby and Double Gloucester.

• **Garlic and peppercorns**. These are the two key ingredients in one of the best flavored cheeses, Gaperon—a white rinded French cheese from the Auvergne.

• **Cumin and caraway seeds**. Simple but effective additions to fine Dutch cheeses such as Leiden and Gouda.

• **Truffles** are a glorious addition to cheese—as they are to anything else. The Italians do it best. Look out for the Caprini Tartufo from Piedmont.

• **Smoked cheeses**. If you like other smoked foods you'll enjoy smoked cheeses, though not everyone feels the natural flavor of a good cheese should be masked by bonfire aromas. Smoked mozzarella, or scamorza, is worth trying.

MAROILLES

CAPRINI TARTUFO

BUYING CHEESE

Given that cheese is one of the few products you can taste before buying, it makes sense to buy it from a specialty store or a cheese department that will readily offer you samples to try.

Good food stores and delis have knowledgeable and enthusiastic staff who can tell you which cheeses are at their best and in season, how they're made, where they come from, and how best to combine them on a cheeseboard. That's not to say that an independent store is automatically better than a supermarket. Some make the mistake of having too big a selection so that the turnover is slow and the cheeses remain on the counter for too long. The very best cheese shops actually mature the cheeses "in-house" so they are sold in the peak of condition.

If you buy from a cheese shop regularly, they'll become aware of your preferences and should instantly be able to suggest cheeses that you will enjoy. Many also operate a mail-order or Internet-based delivery service so you can order cheese from a good shop even if you don't live in the area. But don't ever pass up the opportunity to go and taste in person. It's the best way to find out about cheese!

FARMERS' MARKETS

With cheese, as with every other kind of product, a farmers' market gives you the opportunity to buy from the producer directly. You'll never have the choice that you get in a cheese shop or supermarket but there's a great deal of pleasure in getting to know a producer well and tracking how their cheese changes through the seasons. Very often it's the simplest cheeses that are best bought this way—young goat cheese just a couple of days old can be truly delicious.

SUPERMARKETS

It's hard to fault supermarkets on their range of cheeses these days. Even though some can be very bland, other cheeses can be as good as you'd find in a specialty shop. The downside is that you can't taste before you buy, so it can be difficult to know whether a cheese is ready to eat. With softer examples like Brie, the best way to test is to press the center of the cheese gently with the ball of your thumb. It should be beginning to soften.

HOW MUCH CHEESE TO BUY?

Obviously it depends upon how much cheese you eat, but it's better to buy no more than you are likely to consume over the next couple of days. Treat cheese like any other fresh produce such as meat and fish, rather than simply as something to keep on hand (see page 20).

STORING

The two main enemies of cheese are excessive heat and air. Heat makes it deteriorate rapidly. Leaving it open to air will dry it out and leave it prey to the bacteria that cause mold.

The ideal conditions are those found in a good cheese shop—cool and slightly humid, but many of us do not have access to a cool pantry. That leaves the refrigerator as the only realistic possibility; but preferably store it in a warmer part. Check the manufacturer's instruction booklet for advice.

You need to wrap the cheese properly. The original wrapping—whether it's a tub, a wooden box, or waxed paper—is the best option, but if you open a cheese that's been vacuum packed or have to re-wrap a cheese, waxed paper or foil is generally better than plastic wrap, which can make the cheese moist and sweaty. However, plastic wrap is an acceptable way of wrapping blue cheeses and hard grating cheeses like Parmesan. Beware of putting cheeses together in a plastic container since milder cheeses may pick up flavors from stronger ones.

It's advisable not to keep cheeses too long once you cut into them. Softer cheeses and those that have already been matured by a cheese shop will deteriorate faster than harder ones, and should ideally be consumed within one to two days. If you keep them for longer, re-wrap them regularly.

Can you freeze cheese? Purists would say no, but if you have more cheese left over than you are able to eat immediately, it makes sense, though be prepared for a loss of quality. Hard cheeses generally freeze better than softer ones. Grating them first makes them easier to use.

SERVING RULES

The most important thing when serving cheese is to remember to take it out of the refrigerator at least an hour ahead of serving it. You only get the full flavor from it when it's at room temperature. You should also wait to cut it up until just before serving, because from the moment it's cut, cheese begins to dry out.

When serving a selection of cheeses on a cheeseboard, ideally you should provide a different knife for each type of cheese. That way you avoid smearing soft cheeses on hard ones or mingling strong cheeses with mild ones. For a more informal occasion, like a picnic, use a napkin to wipe the knife before cutting each cheese. You can buy special cheese knives with holes in them that make it easier to cut through softer cheeses such as Camembert or Pont l'Evêque. Cheese slicers are a useful tool when you want to cut thin slices for sandwiches.

When you cut from a cheese that's already been cut in a wedge, try to cut a long thin slice along the edge of the cheese rather than simply cutting off the tip of the wedge. Smaller, circular cheeses can be cut into wedges, while harder cheeses like pecorino taste better cut into thin slices rather than into chunks or cubes. Grating cheeses like Parmesan should always be grated just before serving.

Don't remove the rind from a cheese before serving it, even though you may not want to eat it. Whether you choose to eat a rind or not is a question of taste rather than safety, though most people would be inclined to discard harder rinds or the rinds of pungent cheeses which can be stronger than the cheese itself. Obviously don't eat a waxed rind.

CLOCKWISE FROM BACK: HARBOURNE BLUE,
MONTGOMERY'S CHEDDAR, EXPLORATEUR,
SARIETTE DE BANON, SAINT FÉLICIEN

CHEESEBOARDS

If you're serving cheese to guests you'll generally want to offer some choice. Not everyone likes—or can eat—the same kind of cheese. Some are intolerant of cow's milk for instance. Others can't stand strong blues. Ardent cheese lovers really appreciate the interplay of colors, shapes, and flavors you get with a selection of different cheeses.

While you can theme a cheeseboard—all Italian cheeses, say, or all goat's milk cheeses—most people tend to opt for a board that reflects cheeses of different origin, flavor, and texture. You will probably want to include (though there may be some overlap between these categories):

- A sheep's and/or a goat cheese as well as cow's milk cheeses.
- Cheeses from more than one country.
- A range of textures—from soft and creamy to hard.
- A variety of flavors—from mild to strong.
- A selection of colors. It would be normal to include at least one blue. Washed rind cheeses always look colorful, too.
- Different shapes and sizes, from circular cheeses to wedges.

For example, your cheeseboard might feature a local young goat cheese bought from the farmers' market, a small washed rind cheese such as Saint Marcellin, a wedge of sharp Cheddar, and a blue sheep's milk cheese (see page 14). Or if you wanted to compare and contrast different cheeses, you could pick three cheeses of the same type—say, three sheep's milk varieties, or three different blues.

PRESENTING THE CHEESE

Conventionally, cheeses tend to be arranged on a wooden board or marble slab but slate can also look attractive. A shallow wicker basket will give a rustic feel, but in general it's better for the surface to be flat to make cutting easier. Alternatively, you could plate the cheeses for each person as they do in restaurants. The conventional way to arrange them is to progress clockwise from soft to hard and mild to strong, but you could break from that by presenting the cheese with different accompaniments. Those that go well with a range of cheeses include grapes, fresh medjool dates, quince paste (*membrillo*), walnuts, and pecans. You'll also want some kind of bread or crackers (see pages 112–21).

ORDERING CHEESE IN A RESTAURANT

What should be a pleasure for cheese lovers can sometimes seem more like a test as the waiter stands expectantly while you select from the 30-odd cheeses being offered. In fact the waiter will probably be delighted if you give him or her the chance to show off some expertise. Although you may want to avoid certain styles of cheeses you know you don't enjoy, use it as a chance to experiment.

HOW MUCH TO SERVE?

It depends upon the role the cheeseboard plays in the meal. If it's the entrée following a soup or a salad, or the focus of a party, allow 6 oz. per person. If it follows the entrée and precedes a dessert, 3 oz. for each person should be ample.

Simply irresistible …
Brie and cherries. That simple. That good.

CHEESE PLATES

The cheese plate is for the cheese lover who likes
to partner a cheese with a perfect accompaniment.
They've become a fashionable way to round off
a meal, but can equally well be served as a light
lunch, a small supper, or a quick snack.

LIGHT LUNCHES

Here are some suggestions for cheese plates that could be served for a light lunch or snack. See also the Snacks and Appetizers recipes on pages 30–51.

• **Summer perfection**. Fresh moussey goat cheese with a delicate herb salad—include chervil, flat-leaf parsley, chives, and maybe a few edible flowers. Season lightly with freshly ground black pepper, sea salt, and a mild olive oil.

• **A traditional ploughman's lunch**. Real farmhouse Cheddar, homemade chutney (see page 122), a good apple, and some home-baked crusty bread (see pages 116–119).

• **An unbeatable classic**. Slices of milky *mozzarella di bufala*, ripe tomatoes, and torn basil, seasoned with freshly ground black pepper, and drizzled with olive oil.

• **Tapas-style**. Nibble some Spanish Manchego cheese with a few slices of Serrano ham, some fat green olives, and roasted almonds.

• **Italian sophistication**. Thin shavings of Parmesan are amazing with raw vegetables such as new season fava beans or very thin slices of raw fennel dressed with olive oil.

• **Beautiful colors, fabulous flavors**. Chunks of watermelon and feta, drizzled with extra virgin olive oil. Grind over them a little black pepper and sprinkle a few pumpkin seeds around the plate.

TO ROUND OFF A MEAL

Cheese can be served French-style, in between an entrée and dessert, or UK-style: after dessert. Fruit—both fresh and dried—is fabulous with cheese, particularly apples and pears. So, more surprisingly, is honey (see also Sweet Cheese page 127).

• **Fresh figs and Gorgonzola**. Simply made for each other, but you do need perfectly ripe juicy figs and a perfectly matured, not overripe cheese.

• French **Munster with caraway seeds**. This is a classic combination from Alsace that can be strangely addictive.

• **Cashel Blue with chestnut honey and roasted chestnuts** makes the perfect winter treat.

• **Pear, Stilton, and walnuts**. The walnuts should be freshly shelled or toasted. The pears could also be poached in red wine.

• **A fruity French "Abbaye" cheese** with unsalted Normandy butter and cider jelly.

• **Spanish Manchego with** *membrillo*. The country's best known sheep's cheese with its delectable quince paste.

GRILLED GOAT CHEESE WITH HERB SALAD

FETA AND WATERMELON SALAD

CHEESE AND WINE

A chunk of cheese, a hunk of freshly baked crusty bread, a glass of wine—the perfect impromptu lunch.

So why is drinking your favorite wine with cheese so often a disappointment? The usual answer is that we're too ambitious, laying out too many different styles of cheese to give the wine a chance, and we tend to head for red wines when white or even a sweet wine would be a better match. If you do want to drink red with a variety of different cheeses, the best wines to choose are aged Spanish reds like Rioja, mature Italian reds such as Amarone, or older vintages of New World Cabernet Sauvignon and Shiraz that are not too oaky. Or, for a less formal occasion, go for a simple fruity wine such as a Côtes du Rhône. Young tannic reds such as Cabernet are the ones that are most likely to clash. Even then it's worth avoiding cheeses that are bound to cause problems like very strong, salty blues or pungent washed rind cheeses such as Epoisses or Maroilles.

Artisanal cheeses are more demanding than commercially produced cheeses but, if you find the right match, they are more rewarding. If it's the wine you want to show off, choose a single fine cheese that will complement it. Wines and cheeses from the same area tend to go well, for example, Sancerre and Crottin de Chavignol, both from the Loire, and Gewürztraminer and Munster from Alsace.

What to drink with ...

SOFT CHEESES
• Whites often go better than reds.
• Try Sauvignon Blanc with goat cheese and garlic-flavored roulés.
• Soft fruity reds like Pinot Noir and Merlot go well with white rinded cheeses like Brie and rich creamy ones like Explorateur.

BLUE CHEESES
• In general, sweet wines work best, though a full-bodied fruity red like Zinfandel can be enjoyable in the same way as port. Hungarian Tokaji is also good.

HARD CHEESES
• Probably the easiest type of cheese to pair with a good red, though some alpine cheeses such as Beaufort are equally enjoyable with a very dry white.
• Mature Gouda and Cheddar-style cheeses and hard sheep's milk cheeses are the kindest to fine wines like red Bordeaux and other top Cabernets. Or even a sliver of Parmesan. Milder English regional cheeses such as Cheshire or Caerphilly can be enjoyable with an English white wine or Sauvignon Blanc.

STRONG CHEESES
• Any cheese that has been matured to the extent that its flavor and aroma are really pungent is likely to cause problems, whether it's a notoriously strong cheese like Epoisses or a normally mild one like Brie. Aromatic whites such as Alsace Gewürztraminer and Tokay Pinot Gris are most likely to work.
• A less conventional but surprisingly successful solution is a Belgian or northern French Trappist-style beer such as Chimay Bleu or a Marc de Champagne.

BEFORE OR AFTER DESSERT?

Up to you. If you're drinking a fine red with your entrée, you may want to follow with cheese as the French do, but if you prefer to finish the meal on a savory note, or with a fortified wine like port, save the cheeseboard until the end of the meal.

COOKING CHEESE

Almost any cheese can be used in cooking but some are more suited to it than others. In general, harder cheeses melt better, though you can broil or bake softer ones such as goat cheese and Camembert.

GRATING

Finely grated Parmigiano-Reggiano is the perfect cheese for sprinkling over pasta or other cooked dishes. It also combines well with bread crumbs to make a crusty topping or coating.

MELTING

Cheddar and Cheddar-style cheeses are the most flexible and flavorsome to use for sauces and toppings, though other English regional cheeses melt well too. Use stronger flavored cheeses rather than milder ones as you will need less, which makes the sauce lighter. Blue cheeses such as Gorgonzola can work well in sauces too, but use them in moderation since cooking intensifies their flavor. Mozzarella is, of course, the traditional cheese for topping pizza (see page 81), and Gruyère and Emmental for fondue (see pages 86 and 91).

BAKING

Soft cheeses such as Camembert, Brie, and Vacherin Mont d'Or can be baked whole in a medium oven—an instant fondue.

SAUTÉING

Works well with slightly elastic cheeses such as haloumi and mozzarella, which makes a delicious fried sandwich (see Mozzarella in Carrozza, page 33).

BROILING

Small goat cheeses (crottins) or slices of a goat cheese log broil wonderfully—an easy appetizer with a few lightly dressed salad greens.

STUFFING

Soft cheeses such as cream cheese or ricotta can be combined with fresh herbs or greens to stuff a chicken, or as a filling for ravioli or lasagne (see page 71).

COOKING TIPS

• Unless you are baking a whole cheese, cut the rind off prior to using the cheese in a recipe, and cut it into thin slices or grate it so that it melts quickly.

• Cheese is easier to grate or slice straight from the refrigerator, but, after grating, let the cheese come to room temperature before adding it to a dish.

• If you're adding cheese to a sauce, remove the sauce from the heat first, before adding the cheese bit by bit until it has melted. If necessary, reheat the sauce just enough to melt the cheese completely. Cheese cooked too long or at too high a temperature will become rubbery and stringy.

SNACKS & APPETIZERS

Even if you're in a hurry, you can whip up a fabulous meal with cheese. Whether it's a homey snack like Rarebit or Cheese on Toast, or the oozily tempting Mozzarella in Carrozza, or a sophisticated and stylish appetizer such as Prosciutto-wrapped Bocconcini Crostini, cheese always hits the spot. Experiment with the way other countries serve cheese, too, like the Greeks' *saganaki* (Sautéed Greek Cheese) or Spanish Eggplant Cheese Fritters— a typical Spanish *tapa*. Take this opportunity to explore the world through cheese.

You'll never make enough of these thin, crunchy savory chips—the secret is not to cook them for too long. They are sometimes made in a skillet, but it is much easier to bake them in quantity in the oven. They keep well in an airtight container. Instead of the Parmesan, you can use Grana Padano for this—it is cheaper and works just as well.

PARMESAN CHIPS

4 oz. freshly grated Grana Padano or Parmesan cheese, about 2 cups

a few fennel seeds (optional)

1 red chile, seeded and finely chopped (optional)

a baking tray

Serves 4

Line a baking tray with nonstick baking parchment. Spoon small mounds of grated cheese onto the paper at regular intervals. Flatten with the back of the spoon. Sprinkle a few fennel seeds or some chopped red chile on top, if using.

Bake in a preheated oven at 400°F for 3 to 6 minutes until golden. Remove from the oven and leave for a couple of minutes to set. You can curl them over a wooden spoon handle or rolling pin at this stage to give a more interesting shape, if you like. Carefully lift them off the paper and transfer to a wire rack to cool completely. These chips will keep for up to 4 days if stored in an airtight container.

MOZZARELLA
IN CARROZZA

18 oz. mozzarella cheese,
thickly sliced

8 thin oval slices of country bread

8 sun-dried tomatoes, soaked until
soft and cut into strips

8 anchovy fillets in oil, drained

2 teaspoons dried oregano

3 eggs, beaten

vegetable oil, for shallow frying

sea salt and freshly ground black pepper

Serves 4

Arrange the mozzarella slices over 4 of the slices of bread. Sprinkle the sun-dried tomatoes, anchovy fillets, and oregano over the mozzarella. Season well with salt and pepper, then put the remaining bread slices on top. Press down well.

Pour the beaten eggs into a large dish and dip the sandwiches in the egg, turning once to coat both sides. Leave them in the egg for 30 minutes to soak it up.

Heat the oil in a deep skillet until a crumb dropped in sizzles instantly. Fry each sandwich for 1 to 2 minutes on each side until crisp and golden brown. Drain on paper towels and serve piping hot.

Although often served towards the end of a Greek meal (like an English cheese savory used to be), this dish may also be served as an appetizer, part of a meze (literally, a "tableful"). Unlike the Cypriot version, which uses local haloumi cheese, the traditional saganaki uses strongly flavored, hard, dry, seasonal cheese such as kefalotyri. If unavailable, use sharp Cheddar instead. Traditionally this is served in small, two-handled skillets brought, sizzling, to the table. The cheese is eaten with a fork or scooped onto crusty bread. Use best-quality olive oil: its taste makes a considerable difference.

SAUTÉED GREEK CHEESE

4 slices kefalotyri cheese or sharp Cheddar, cut ¼-inch thick

all-purpose flour, for dusting

cold-pressed extra virgin olive oil, for cooking (preferably Greek)

coarsely ground black pepper

lemon wedges, to serve

Serves 4

Dust each slice of cheese generously with flour, patting it all over. Heat 2 teaspoons olive oil for each piece of cheese (cook them singly or in pairs, depending on the size of the pan) in a small skillet until very hot. Using tongs, add 1 to 2 slices of floured cheese. Sauté for 1 to 1½ minutes or until golden, crusty, and aromatic and starting to soften inside.

Using a narrow spatula, carefully turn each piece over. Sauté for another 45 seconds on the second side until crusty.

Serve directly from the skillet, adding black pepper and a wedge of lemon, or slide onto a small plate. Continue until all the cheese is cooked. Eat while still hot, crusty, fragrant, and starting to melt.

This is one of those dishes that's perfect for a late-night snack—quick, delicious, and dishwashing-free. It tastes great with any chutney or relish. Be ready to provide seconds.

2 thick slices of white bread

4 oz. cheese, such as Cheddar, a soft creamy goat cheese, or Brie

a few drops of Worcestershire sauce (optional)

pickles, relish, or chutney, to serve

Serves 2

CHEESE ON TOAST

Toast the bread under the broiler on one side only. Grate the cheese onto the untoasted side of the bread (if using very soft cheese, slice it instead). Add a few drops of Worcestershire sauce, if using, and cook under a preheated hot broiler for 2 to 3 minutes until melted and bubbling.

Serve on a platter with the bottle of pickles, relish, or chutney, and a spoon so that guests can help themselves.

"Welsh rabbit"—also known as rarebit—is a glorified version of cheese on toast. It dates back to the mid-sixteenth century, but over time has evolved into countless variations. If you fancy a comforting snack or something light for brunch, lunch, or supper, this easy-to-make rarebit is hard to beat.

RAREBIT

Melt the butter in a heavy saucepan, add the shallots or onion, and cook until softened. Add the cheese, beer, mustard, and salt. Stir over low heat until the cheese has melted. Add the beaten eggs and stir until the mixture has thickened slightly, 2 to 3 minutes. Don't overcook or you will end up with scrambled eggs. Toast the bread on both sides, then spoon the cheese mixture onto the toast and cook under a preheated hot broiler, until puffed and gold-flecked. Serve with lots of black pepper.

2 tablespoons butter

4 shallots or 1 onion, sliced

1 cup grated Cheddar or Gruyère cheese

¼ cup beer

1 teaspoon mustard

a pinch of sea salt

2 eggs, lightly beaten

4 slices of bread

freshly ground black pepper

Serves 2–4

PEAR, PECORINO, AND PEA CROSTINI

1 thin French baguette, cut into thin slices

extra virgin olive oil, for brushing and moistening

2 cups shelled fresh or frozen peas, about 8 oz.

freshly grated nutmeg

1 small ripe pear, cored and finely chopped

a drop of balsamic or sherry vinegar

4 oz. fresh young pecorino or Parmesan cheese, diced, about 1 cup

sea salt and freshly ground black pepper

a baking tray

Serves 6

To make the crostini, brush both sides of each slice of bread with olive oil, and spread out on a baking tray. Bake in a preheated oven at 375°F for about 10 minutes until crisp and golden.

Meanwhile, blanch the peas in boiling water for 3 minutes if they are fresh, or 2 minutes if they are frozen. Drain them, refresh in cold water, and drain again. Put the peas in a food processor or blender and blend to a purée, moistening with a little olive oil. Season with salt, pepper, and freshly grated nutmeg.

Put the pear in a bowl, add a drop of balsamic or sherry vinegar, then add the cheese, and mix well. Spread the crostini with a mound of pea purée and top with a spoonful of the pear and cheese mixture. Serve immediately.

These are delicious mouthfuls of melting mozzarella swathed in prosciutto. They taste good served cold with the addition of a thin slice of ripe melon on top, but heating them up transforms them.

PROSCIUTTO-WRAPPED BOCCONCINI CROSTINI

To make the crostini, brush both sides of each slice of bread with olive oil, and spread out on a baking tray. Bake in a preheated oven at 375°F for about 10 minutes until crisp and golden. Let cool, then keep in an airtight container until ready to use. It is best to reheat them in the oven before adding the topping.

Put a sage leaf on top of each bocconcini or mozzarella cube and season with salt and pepper. Cut each slice of ham into three equal pieces and wrap up a piece of cheese in each one.

Mix the mustard and balsamic vinegar together and spread it on the crostini. Put two wrapped mozzarellas on top of each crostini and put on a baking tray. Return to the oven for 3 to 5 minutes or until the cheese just melts. Serve immediately, topped with more sage leaves.

1 thin French baguette, cut into thin slices

extra virgin olive oil, for brushing

24 fresh sage leaves, plus extra to serve

24 bocconcini cheeses or 26 oz. mozzarella cheese, cubed

8 slices of prosciutto

3 tablespoons whole-grain mustard

1 teaspoon balsamic vinegar

sea salt and freshly ground black pepper

a baking tray

Serves 6

Served warm, these soufflés are an easy appetizer, because you don't have to panic getting them to the table before they sink! Make sure you butter the ramekins very well so that you can get the soufflés out easily.

WARM GOAT CHEESE SOUFFLÉS

2 tablespoons unsalted butter

2 tablespoons all-purpose flour

1 cup milk

4 oz. soft goat cheese

3 eggs, separated

2 tablespoons chopped fresh mixed herbs, such as basil, chives, mint, and tarragon

sea salt and freshly ground black pepper

arugula salad, to serve

6 ramekins, 1 cup each, well buttered

Serves 6

Melt the butter in a saucepan, add the flour, and cook over low heat for 30 seconds. Remove the pan from the heat and gradually stir in the milk until smooth. Return to the heat and stir constantly until the mixture thickens. Cook for 1 minute.

Let cool slightly, then beat in the cheese, egg yolks, herbs, salt, and pepper. Put the egg whites in a bowl and beat until soft peaks form. Fold the egg whites into the cheese mixture.

Spoon the mixture into the prepared ramekins and bake in a preheated oven at 400°F for 15 to 18 minutes until risen and golden on top. Remove from the oven and let cool for about 15 minutes.

Using a spatula, work around the edges of the soufflés and turn them out onto plates. Serve with arugula salad.

4 thick slices of goat cheese with rind
(Bûcheron), 2 oz. each

extra virgin olive oil, for sprinkling

1 tablespoon chopped fresh thyme

freshly ground black pepper

TO SERVE

4 slices of sourdough bread

1–2 garlic cloves, halved

green salad

a baking tray, lined with foil

Serves 4

BAKED CHÈVRE

Put the slices of goat cheese on the prepared baking tray, sprinkle
with a little oil, dot with thyme leaves, and season with pepper.
Bake in a preheated oven at 400°F for 10 to 12 minutes until just
starting to ooze and run.

Meanwhile, toast the sourdough, then rub it with the cut side of the
garlic. When the cheese is ready, spread it onto the toasted, garlicky
sourdough and serve with a green salad.

This tapas-type dish is sometimes found in bars in Barcelona and elsewhere in Spain served with the local rosé or red wine, well chilled: a delicious combination. If you can't find Spanish Cabrales cheese, use a sharp Cheddar.

EGGPLANT CHEESE FRITTERS

1 large eggplant, about 12 oz.

6–7 oz. strong, meltable cheese such as Cabrales or sharp Cheddar

⅔ cup all-purpose flour, seasoned with salt and pepper

2 eggs, well beaten with a fork

about 2 cups virgin olive oil or safflower oil, for frying

SALSA

2 medium vine-ripened tomatoes, roughly chopped

¼ cup chile oil, or olive oil mixed with ½ teaspoon Tabasco sauce

4 teaspoons red wine vinegar or sherry vinegar

12 fresh basil leaves

sea salt and freshly ground black pepper

about 12 wooden toothpicks

an electric deep-fat fryer (optional)

Serves 4

Using a sharp, serrated knife, cut the eggplant crosswise into 18 to 24 thin slices about ¼ inch thick. Slice the cheese into pieces of the same thickness. Cut and piece them together to fit, sandwiching a slice of cheese between 2 slices of eggplant. To keep the "sandwiches" closed during cooking, push a wooden toothpick, at an angle, through each one.

Put the flour on a plate. Pour the beaten eggs into a shallow dish. Dip the eggplant "sandwiches" first into the flour, then into the beaten eggs, then in flour again to coat well all over.

Fill a deep skillet one-third full with the oil, or an electric deep-fat fryer to the manufacturer's recommended level. Heat to 375°F or until a ½-inch cube of bread browns in 30 seconds. Slide some of the prepared "sandwiches" into the hot oil in batches of 3 and fry for 2 to 3 minutes on the first side. Using tongs, turn and cook for 1 to 2 minutes on the other side or until golden and crisp, with the cheese melting inside. Drain on crumpled paper towels while you coat and cook the rest.

Meanwhile, to make the salsa, put the tomatoes, chile oil, vinegar, basil leaves, salt, and pepper in a food processor. Pulse in brief bursts to a coarse mixture.

Serve the fritters hot with a trickle of the salsa, or with a little container of salsa as a dip at the side of the plate.

These rolls are a fabulous addition to any array of fingerfood or can be served as an appetizer. They may seem complicated, but there are many ways to make them simpler: buy the tapenade or make it up a couple of weeks in advance, roast and peel the peppers the night before, then assemble the rolls in advance.

ROASTED RED BELL PEPPER AND GOAT CHEESE ROLLS

4 red bell peppers, cut in half, seeded, and white membranes removed

olive oil, for sprinkling

6 oz. goat cheese, soft or firm, but not hard

a handful of fresh basil leaves

sprigs of rosemary, to serve (optional)

OLIVE TAPENADE

1 cup black olives, such as Niçoise or Kalamata, pitted

¼ cup olive oil

2 tablespoons capers, rinsed and drained

a baking tray

Makes 16

Put the bell peppers on the baking tray and sprinkle with olive oil. Roast in a preheated oven at 425°F for about 30 minutes until charred and blistered. Remove from the oven and cover with a damp dishtowel. Set aside for 5 to 10 minutes to steam off the skins—this makes peeling much easier.

Meanwhile, to make the olive tapenade, put the olives, olive oil, and capers in a blender and blend to a fairly coarse mixture.

Carefully remove the skins from the bell peppers, making sure you don't tear the flesh, then cut each piece in half again. Put each piece of pepper, skinned side down, on a work surface, then smear generously with the tapenade. Add a small piece of goat cheese and a few basil leaves. Carefully roll up the filled pepper, then put, seam side down, on a serving platter. Secure with a sprig of rosemary, if using, then serve.

COOK'S TIPS
Don't overfill the peppers—any remaining tapenade can be put in a screw-top bottle, covered with a thin layer of olive oil, and stored in the refrigerator for 2 to 3 weeks.

The rosemary skewers not only look good, but they also add flavor to the peppers.

These Italian polenta (cornmeal) rounds are a dream for a party because everything can be made in advance—in fact, if you are super-organized you can make the tapenade a couple of weeks ahead. When serving polenta firm, it is better to leave it overnight to set. You can cut it up and top with the tapenade a few hours before serving. Bring out the colors by serving on a bed of greens such as arugula or watercress.

3 tablespoons unsalted butter

1 tablespoon olive oil

1 garlic clove, crushed

3 scallions, finely chopped

2 oz. plus 2 tablespoons polenta or yellow cornmeal, about ⅓ cup

4 oz. feta cheese, crumbled into small pieces, about 1 cup

a small handful of dill, coarsely chopped

sea salt and freshly ground black pepper

8–16 pitted black olives, sliced, to serve

TOMATO TAPENADE

2 oz. sun dried tomatoes, about ½ cup, soaked overnight in warm water with 1 tablespoon vinegar

⅓ cup olive oil

1 tablespoon balsamic vinegar

½ red serrano chile, seeded

a small handful of fresh basil leaves

a baking pan, 8 inches square, well greased

a cookie cutter, 2 inches diameter

Makes 16

HERB AND FETA POLENTA
topped with sun-dried tomato tapenade

To make the tapenade, put the soaked tomatoes in a blender. Add the olive oil, balsamic vinegar, chile, and basil, then blend until the mixture is fairly smooth.

To make the polenta mixture, put the butter, oil, garlic, and scallions in a saucepan and cook over medium heat for 10 minutes until the onions are translucent. Pour in 1¼ cups boiling water, then add the polenta in a steady stream, whisking all the time to stop lumps forming. Continue cooking according to the instructions on the polenta package. Stir in the feta and dill, add salt and pepper to taste, then pour into the prepared pan. Chill in the refrigerator overnight.

Cut out 16 polenta rounds with the cookie cutter. Top each round with a generous spoonful of tapenade and a few slices of black olives, then serve.

COOK'S TIP
To store the tapenade, put it in a screw-top bottle and cover with a thin layer of olive oil. Keep in the refrigerator for 2 to 3 weeks.

The tapenade also makes a good crostini topping or a pasta sauce.

These pastries offer a lovely array of tastes and textures—the spinach provides a neutral backdrop for the rich cheese, sweet fruit, and crunchy pine nuts, all wrapped up in a crisp phyllo shell. They make quite a sensation—and also freeze superbly.

SPINACH AND BLUE CHEESE PHYLLO PASTRIES

with apricots and pine nuts

1 tablespoon olive oil

12 oz. spinach, washed well

½ teaspoon ground nutmeg

1 garlic clove, crushed

a small handful of fresh dill, coarsely chopped

6 oz. blue cheese, such as dolcelatte, cut into small cubes, 1½–2 cups

3–4 dried apricots, about 2 oz., soaked overnight, drained, and sliced

½ cup pine nuts, toasted in a dry skillet until golden

8 oz. phyllo pastry dough (½ package)

olive oil or melted butter, for brushing

sea salt and freshly ground black pepper

crisp salad greens, to serve (optional)

a baking tray, lightly oiled

Makes 6 rolls

Heat the oil in a wok or skillet over medium heat. Add the spinach, nutmeg, and garlic and stir-fry until the spinach has just wilted. Scoop into a colander to drain. Let cool, then squeeze out the liquid with the back of a spoon. Put the spinach mixture in a bowl and add the dill, blue cheese, apricots, pine nuts, and salt and pepper to taste.

Cut 2 sheets of the phyllo dough to about 12 x 6 inches. Put 1 sheet on the counter and brush with oil or melted butter. Put the second sheet on top. Divide the filling into 6 portions. Spoon 1 portion along the narrow edge and firmly roll up the double layer of dough, tucking in the ends as you go. Repeat until all the filling has been used and you have 6 rolls.

Transfer the rolls to the prepared baking tray and bake in a preheated oven at 350°F for 25 minutes, then turn over and cook for another 15 minutes. Serve 1 roll per person, with a few crisp salad greens, if using.

SALADS & VEGETABLES

Cheese is a great partner for all kinds of raw and cooked vegetables. Crisp, crunchy ones like celery and Belgian endive provide perfect textural contrast to a crumbly blue cheese salad, while herbs like mint give a lovely lift to a Zucchini and Feta Salad. And how is it that a simple cheese sauce can elevate a humble cauliflower into the gastronomic superleague? To say nothing of the indulgence of melting Reblochon cheese with potatoes, which makes the satisfyingly rich *tartiflette*.

Developed unintentionally by a gardener at the Brussels botanical gardens in the middle of the nineteenth century, Belgian endive is now cultivated for a good part of the year, and modern varieties have none of the bitterness of their ancestors. When buying, choose very pale endives with only a hint of green; they grow in the dark, so color on the leaves is a sign that they have been exposed to the light and are not as fresh. Also, big is not necessarily better; 8 inches is the maximum length for best taste.

BELGIAN ENDIVE SALAD WITH ROQUEFORT, CELERY, AND WALNUTS

4–5 heads of Belgian endive, about 1¼ lb., cut in half, cored, and thinly sliced

2 celery stalks, thinly sliced, plus a few leaves, torn

3 oz. Roquefort cheese, crumbled, about ¾ cup

2 oz. shelled walnuts, chopped, about ½ cup

a handful of flat-leaf parsley, finely chopped

1 baguette, sliced, to serve

WALNUT VINAIGRETTE

2 tablespoons wine vinegar

1 teaspoon fine sea salt

1 teaspoon Dijon mustard

7 tablespoons safflower oil (see method)

1 tablespoon walnut oil (optional)

freshly ground black pepper

Serves 4

To prepare the vinaigrette, put the vinegar in the bowl you plan to serve the salad in. Using a fork or a small whisk, beat in the salt until almost dissolved. You may have to tilt the bowl so the vinegar is deep enough to have something to stir. Mix in the mustard until blended. Add the oil, 1 tablespoon at a time, beating well between each addition, until emulsified. If you're using the walnut oil, use 1 less tablespoon of safflower oil. Stir in pepper to taste.

Just before you're ready to serve the salad, add the endive, celery, Roquefort, walnuts, and parsley to the vinaigrette and toss well. Serve immediately, with a basket of sliced baguette.

This refreshing summer salad with a bright note of fresh mint makes a superb accompaniment to grilled meat or fish.

ZUCCHINI, FETA, AND MINT SALAD

1 tablespoon sesame seeds

6 medium zucchini

3 tablespoons extra virgin olive oil

6 oz. feta cheese, crumbled, about 1½ cups

a handful of fresh mint leaves

sea salt and freshly ground black pepper

DRESSING

¼ cup extra virgin olive oil

1 tablespoon freshly squeezed lemon juice

1 small garlic clove, crushed

Serves 4

Put the sesame seeds in a dry skillet and toast over medium heat until golden and aromatic. Remove from the pan, let cool, and set aside until needed.

Preheat the grill. Cut the zucchini diagonally into thick slices, toss with the olive oil, and season with salt and pepper. Cook over hot coals for 2 to 3 minutes on each side until charred and tender. Remove and let cool.

Put all the dressing ingredients in a screw-top jar and shake well. Season to taste with salt and pepper.

Put the zucchini, feta, and mint in a large bowl, add the dressing, and toss well until evenly coated. Sprinkle with the sesame seeds and serve at once.

Fatoush is a bread salad made from grilled pita bread. It's often accompanied by haloumi, a firm cheese that can be grilled. Mozzarella cheese can also be cooked on the grill. It picks up an appealing smokiness in the process.

GRILLED PITA SALAD WITH OLIVE SALSA AND MOZZARELLA

8 oz. mozzarella cheese, drained

¼–⅓ cup extra virgin olive oil, plus extra for brushing

1 large green bell pepper, seeded and diced

1 Lebanese (mini) cucumber, chopped

2 ripe tomatoes, chopped

½ red onion, finely chopped

2 pita breads

freshly squeezed juice of ½ lemon

sea salt and freshly ground black pepper

OLIVE SALSA

⅔ cup Kalamata olives, pitted and chopped

1 tablespoon chopped fresh parsley

1 small garlic clove, finely chopped

¼ cup extra virgin olive oil

1 tablespoon freshly squeezed lemon juice

Serves 4

Wrap the mozzarella in paper towels and squeeze to remove excess water. Unwrap and cut into thick slices. Brush the slices well with olive oil. Cook on a grill over hot coals for 1 minute on each side until the cheese is charred with lines and beginning to soften. Alternatively, simply slice the cheese and use without grilling.

Put the green pepper, cucumber, tomatoes, and onion in a bowl. Toast the pita breads over the hot coals, let cool slightly, then tear into bite-size pieces. Add to the bowl, then pour a spoonful or two of the olive oil and a little lemon juice over them. Season with salt and pepper and stir well.

To make the olive salsa, put the olives, parsley, garlic, oil, and lemon juice in a bowl and stir well. Season to taste with pepper.

Spoon the salad onto appetizer plates, top with a few slices of mozzarella and some olive salsa, and serve.

A regular accompaniment to entrées in french bistros, this recipe goes especially well with pork. The secret of delicious cauliflower is to blanch it first; if you parboil it with a bay leaf, the unpleasant cabbage aroma disappears.

CAULIFLOWER GRATIN

1 fresh bay leaf

1 large cauliflower, separated into large florets

2 cups heavy cream

1 large egg

2 teaspoons Dijon mustard

6 oz. finely grated Comté cheese, about 1½ cups*

coarse sea salt

a baking dish, about 10 inches diameter, greased with butter

Serves 4–6

Bring a large saucepan of water to a boil, add the bay leaf, salt generously, then add the cauliflower. Cook until still slightly firm, about 10 minutes. Drain and set aside.

Put the cream in a saucepan and bring to a boil. Boil for 10 minutes, then stir in the egg, mustard, and 1 teaspoon of salt.

Divide the cauliflower into smaller florets, then stir into the cream sauce. Transfer to the prepared dish and sprinkle the cheese over the top in an even layer. Bake in a preheated oven at 400°F until golden, 40 to 45 minutes. Serve hot.

*NOTE Like Gruyère, Comté is a mountain cheese—from the Franche-Comté region to be precise—but the similarity stops there. Comté's distinct flavor comes from the milk used in the making, so the flavor varies with the seasons. A springtime diet of tender young shoots delivers milk that is very different from its winter counterpart, when the cows are nourished mainly on hay. In summer, Comté is darker in color and fruitier; in winter, it is paler and more nutty. Use Emmental or Cantal if it is unavailable.

A meal in itself, this is very rich and filling, perfect after a day on the slopes. You might find this on menus in the Savoie region of France, though it is not, strictly speaking, a traditional recipe. It was "invented" in the 1980s by the local cheese committee to help sell more Reblochon cheese. Serve with a mixed green salad.

POTATOES BAKED WITH REBLOCHON CHEESE

2¼ lb. boiling potatoes

1 fresh bay leaf

4 tablespoons unsalted butter

2 onions, cut in half and sliced

5 thick strips of bacon, cubed

⅓ cup dry white wine

1 Reblochon cheese, 1 lb.*

coarse sea salt and freshly ground black pepper

a baking dish, about 12 inches long, greased with butter

Serves 6

Put the potatoes in a large saucepan, then add the bay leaf and cold water to cover. Bring to a boil, add some salt, and cook until the potatoes are *al dente*, about 15 minutes. Drain. When cool enough to handle, peel and cut into ¼-inch slices.

Melt half the butter in a sauté pan or skillet, add the onions and bacon, and cook until just browned. Remove with a slotted spoon and set aside. Add the remaining butter and the potatoes and cook gently for 5 minutes. Stir carefully without breaking too many potato slices. Add the wine, bring to a boil, and boil for 1 minute. Season with salt and pepper.

Arrange the potatoes in the prepared baking dish. Scrub the rind of the cheese lightly with a vegetable brush, then cut the cheese into 8 wedges. Cut each piece in half through the middle, so each has skin on one side only. Arrange the cheese pieces on top of the potatoes, skin side up. Cover with foil and bake in a preheated oven at 425°F for about 15 minutes. Remove the foil and bake 15 to 20 minutes more, until browned. Serve hot.

*NOTE If Reblochon is unavailable, substitute any other French mountain cheese, such as Emmental, Cantal, or a Pyrénées. A firm goat cheese, such as Crottin de Chavignol, also works well served with potatoes in this way. Alternatively, this recipe is a great way to clear out a cluttered cheese compartment, especially the post-dinner party syndrome of lovely but unfinished cheeses. Simply crumble or slice whatever you've got on top of the potatoes before baking.

PASTA, PIZZA, & RISOTTO

Think of Italy and you think of Parmesan and all the dishes it adorns—pasta, pizza, and risotto. But there are other, less usual ways of topping these much-loved dishes for instance with salsa verde and grilled cheeses, prosciutto and Cambozola, or mushrooms and mascarpone. Don't be afraid to try less familiar Italian cheeses such as fontina and Taleggio, both of which melt beautifully, or wonderful, tangy Gorgonzola with its fabulously creamy texture. Not to mention that other great Italian classic, buffalo mozzarella, bought fresh and milky straight from the deli.

You can vary this salsa verde each time you make it, according to the herbs you have at hand—parsley should always be the base, but feel free to add others such as basil, tarragon, or mint instead of the cilantro.

FUSILLI WITH SALSA VERDE AND CHAR-GRILLED CHEESE

10 oz. dried pasta, such as fusilli, about 4 cups

1 tablespoon olive oil

2 tablespoons all-purpose flour

1 teaspoon cracked black pepper

8 oz. cheese, such as haloumi or provolone, cut into ¼-inch slices

sea salt

SALSA VERDE

2 anchovy fillets in oil, drained

1 tablespoon salted capers, rinsed well

1 green chile, seeded and finely chopped

1 garlic clove, crushed

3 tablespoons chopped fresh flat-leaf parsley

1 tablespoon chopped fresh cilantro

2 teaspoons Dijon mustard

3 tablespoons olive oil

1 tablespoon white wine vinegar

Serves 4

Bring a large saucepan of water to a boil. Add a good pinch of salt, then the pasta, and cook until *al dente*, or according to the timings on the package.

Meanwhile, to make the salsa verde, put the anchovy fillets and capers onto a cutting board and, using a heavy knife, chop finely. Put the chile and garlic on top and chop again until very finely chopped. Transfer to a bowl and add the herbs, mustard, olive oil, and vinegar.

Heat 1 tablespoon oil in a stove-top grill pan until hot. Put the flour onto a small plate, add the black pepper, and mix. Dip each cheese slice in the flour to coat on both sides, shaking off any excess. Cook on the grill pan for 1 to 2 minutes on each side until golden brown, then remove and drain on paper towels.

Drain the pasta well and return it to the warm pan. Add the salsa verde and toss to mix. Divide between 4 bowls or plates, arrange the cheese on top, then serve.

A simplified version of that old-time favorite, macaroni and cheese, but with no flour and no risk of lumps.

THREE CHEESE BAKED PENNE

12 oz. dried pasta, such as penne, about 4½ cups

2 cups mascarpone cheese

2 tablespoons whole-grain mustard

10 oz. fontina cheese, grated

¼ cup freshly grated Parmesan cheese

sea salt and freshly ground black pepper

a baking dish, about 12 x 8 inches

Serves 4

Bring a large saucepan of water to a boil. Add a good pinch of salt, then the pasta, and cook until *al dente*, or according to the timings on the package.

Drain the pasta well and return it to the warm pan. Add the mascarpone and stir. Add the mustard, fontina, and Parmesan, with salt and pepper to taste. Stir to mix.

Transfer to the baking dish and cook in a preheated oven at 400°F for 25 to 30 minutes until golden and bubbling. Serve immediately.

GREEN LASAGNE WITH RICOTTA PESTO AND MUSHROOMS

8 oz. fresh spinach lasagne or 1 package dried spinach lasagne

MUSHROOM SAUCE

1 oz. dried porcini mushrooms, soaked in warm water for 20 minutes

¼ cup olive oil

4 tablespoons unsalted butter

2 lb. fresh wild mushrooms or portobellos, thinly sliced

1 onion, chopped

4 garlic cloves, chopped

¼ cup chopped fresh flat-leaf parsley

2–3 sprigs of thyme, chopped

1¼ cups chicken or vegetable broth

RICOTTA PESTO

3 garlic cloves

¾ cup pine nuts

3½ cups fresh basil leaves

⅔ cup olive oil

6 tablespoons unsalted butter, softened, plus extra to serve

¼ cup freshly grated Parmesan cheese, plus extra for sprinkling

1 cup fresh ricotta cheese

sea salt and freshly ground black pepper

an ovenproof dish, 12 x 9 x 2 inches, buttered

Serves 6

To make the mushroom sauce, drain the soaked mushrooms, reserving the soaking liquid. Squeeze them gently, then chop coarsely. Heat half the oil and all the butter in a large skillet. When foaming, add half the chopped soaked mushrooms, half the fresh mushrooms, and half the onion. Sauté over high heat for 4 to 5 minutes until tender, then remove from the pan. Repeat with the remaining mushrooms and onions, then mix the 2 batches in the pan. Stir in the garlic, parsley, and thyme and cook for 2 minutes. Add the stock and soaking liquid, then boil for 4 to 5 minutes until the sauce is syrupy. Remove from the heat and let cool.

To make the pesto, pound the garlic, pine nuts, and a sprinkling of salt with a mortar and pestle. Add the basil leaves, a few at a time, pounding to a paste. Transfer to a bowl and gradually beat in the olive oil until creamy. Beat in the butter, season with pepper, then beat in the Parmesan. Alternatively, put everything in a food processor and blend until smooth. Transfer to a bowl, add the ricotta, and stir well.

Bring a large saucepan of salted water to a boil and drop in a few lasagne sheets at a time. Fresh pasta is cooked when the water returns to a boil. Lift it out and drain over the sides of a colander. If using dried lasagne, follow the instructions on the package.

Line the prepared dish with a layer of lasagne and add a layer of ricotta pesto. Add another layer of pasta, a layer of mushroom sauce, then a layer of lasagne. Repeat until all the ingredients have been used, finishing with a layer of lasagne. Sprinkle with Parmesan and dot with butter.

Cover with oiled aluminum foil and bake in a preheated oven at 350°F for 20 minutes. Uncover, then bake for another 20 minutes until golden. Let stand for 10 minutes before serving (this will make it easier to cut).

The prosciutto crisps up beautifully in a nonstick skillet, and forms a delicious, salty contrast to the creamy cheese.

PASTA WITH PROSCIUTTO, ARUGULA, AND BUBBLING BLUE CHEESE

10 oz. dried pasta, such as pappardelle or lasagnette

2 tablespoons olive oil

8 slices of prosciutto

1 pint cherry tomatoes

2 soft blue cheeses, about 5 oz. each

2 tablespoons Marsala wine or sherry

2 tablespoons chopped fresh flat-leaf parsley

a handful of arugula

sea salt and freshly ground black pepper

Serves 4

Bring a large saucepan of water to a boil. Add a good pinch of salt, then the pasta, and cook until *al dente*, or according to the timings on the package.

Meanwhile, heat a little of the oil in a nonstick skillet, add the prosciutto, and cook for 1 minute on each side until crisp. Remove and drain on paper towels. Add the remaining oil to the pan. When hot, add the cherry tomatoes and cook for 3 to 4 minutes until split and softened.

Meanwhile, cut each cheese in half crosswise and put, cut side up, under a hot broiler. Cook for 2 to 3 minutes until golden and bubbling.

Break the prosciutto into pieces and add to the tomatoes in the pan. Add the Marsala or sherry, parsley, and salt and pepper to taste.

Drain the pasta well and return it to the warm pan. Add the prosciutto and tomato mixture and toss gently to mix. Divide between 4 bowls or plates and sprinkle with arugula. Using a spatula, slide a bubbling cheese half on top of each. Sprinkle with black pepper and serve immediately.

Fontina, Gorgonzola, Taleggio, and Parmesan are four of the best Italian cheeses. Try mixing and matching your own selection, but choose ones that are quite creamy and have a good flavor. Use them at room temperature for maximum taste.

RISOTTO WITH FOUR CHEESES

4 cups vegetable broth

4 tablespoons unsalted butter

1 tablespoon olive oil

8 shallots, finely chopped (if unavailable, use ½ cup minced mild onions)

1 garlic clove, crushed

1½ cups risotto rice, such as vialone nano, carnaroli, or arborio

½ cup white wine

1½ cups freshly grated Parmesan cheese, plus extra to serve

2 oz. Gorgonzola cheese, cut into cubes, about ¾ cup

2 oz. fontina cheese, cut into cubes, about ¾ cup

2 oz. Taleggio cheese, rind removed and cheese cut into cubes, about ¾ cup

a handful of fresh flat-leaf parsley, coarsely chopped

sea salt and freshly ground black pepper

Serves 4

Put the broth in a saucepan. Heat until almost boiling, then reduce the heat until barely simmering to keep it hot.

Heat the butter and oil in a deep skillet or heavy saucepan over medium heat. Add the shallots and cook for 1 to 2 minutes until softened but not browned. Add the garlic and mix well.

Add the rice and stir with a wooden spoon until the grains are well coated and glistening, about 1 minute. Pour in the wine and stir until it has been completely absorbed.

Add 1 ladle of hot broth and simmer, stirring until it has been absorbed. Continue to add the broth at intervals and cook as before until the liquid has been absorbed and the rice is tender but still firm (*al dente*), about 18 to 20 minutes. Reserve the last ladle of broth.

Add the reserved broth, the four cheeses, parsley, salt, and pepper. Mix well. Remove from the heat, cover, and let rest for 2 minutes.

Spoon into warmed bowls, sprinkle with grated Parmesan, and serve.

Taleggio—named after a valley in Bergamo where it originates—is made from the milk of cows that graze the Alpine pastures, then the cheese is ripened in caves. Its sweet flavor complements the peppery taste of watercress. Arugula with Taleggio is also delicious.

RISOTTO WITH WATERCRESS AND TALEGGIO

4 cups vegetable broth

6 tablespoons unsalted butter

1 tablespoon olive oil

8 shallots, finely chopped (if unavailable, use ½ cup minced mild onions)

1½ cups risotto rice, such as vialone nano, carnaroli, or arborio

⅓ cup white wine

a bunch of watercress, trimmed and chopped, plus extra leaves to serve

1½ cups freshly grated Parmesan cheese

7 oz. Taleggio cheese, rind removed and cheese cut into cubes, about 2½ cups

sea salt and freshly ground black pepper

Serves 4

Put the broth in a saucepan. Heat until almost boiling, then reduce the heat until barely simmering to keep it hot.

Heat 2 tablespoons of the butter and the oil in a deep skillet or heavy saucepan over medium heat. Add the shallots and cook for 1 to 2 minutes until softened but not browned.

Add the rice and stir with a wooden spoon until the grains are well coated and glistening, about 1 minute. Pour in the wine and stir until it has been completely absorbed.

Add 1 ladle of hot broth and simmer, stirring until it has been absorbed. Repeat with another ladle of broth. After 10 minutes, add the watercress and mix well. Continue to add the broth at intervals and cook as before, for 8 to 10 minutes more until the liquid has been absorbed and the rice is tender but still firm (*al dente*).

Mix in the Parmesan, Taleggio, the remaining butter, salt, and pepper. Remove from the heat, cover, and let rest for 2 minutes.

Spoon into warmed bowls, top with watercress leaves, and serve.

Fontina is a mountain cheese from Lombardy and it is delicately flavored—mild enough not to overpower the walnuts. Fontina can also be used in lasagne, fondue, or melted in a grilled cheese sandwich filled with arugula.

FONTINA AND WALNUT RISOTTO

4 cups vegetable broth

4 tablespoons unsalted butter

1 tablespoon olive oil

8 shallots, finely chopped (if unavailable, use ⅓ cup minced mild onions)

1 garlic clove, crushed

1½ cups risotto rice, such as vialone nano, carnaroli, or arborio

⅓ cup white wine

4 oz. fontina cheese, cut into cubes, about 1⅓ cups

1½ cups freshly grated Parmesan cheese

⅓ cup walnut pieces, coarsely chopped

a handful of fresh flat-leaf parsley, coarsely chopped

sea salt and freshly ground black pepper

TO SERVE (OPTIONAL)

walnut pieces, coarsely chopped

freshly grated Parmesan cheese

Serves 4

Put the stock in a saucepan. Heat until almost boiling, then reduce the heat until barely simmering to keep it hot.

Heat the butter and oil in a sauté pan or other heavy pan over medium heat. Add the shallots and cook for 1 to 2 minutes until softened but not browned. Add the garlic and mix well.

Add the rice and stir, using a wooden spoon until the grains are well coated and glistening, about 1 minute. Pour in the wine and stir until it has been completely absorbed.

Add 1 ladle of hot broth and simmer, stirring until it has been absorbed. Continue to add the broth at intervals and cook as before until the liquid has been absorbed and the rice is tender but still firm (al dente), about 18 to 20 minutes. Reserve the last ladle of broth.

Add the reserved broth, fontina, Parmesan, walnuts, parsley, salt, and pepper. Stir well. Remove from the heat, cover, and let rest for 2 minutes.

Spoon into warmed bowls, sprinkle with walnuts and grated Parmesan, if using, and serve immediately.

If you are really short of time you can cheat a little here and use a 16 oz. pack of frozen pizza dough, cut in half—for two people you will need a whole package. Follow the instructions on the pack but let the dough rise for 15 minutes after rolling it out.

MOZZARELLA PIZZAS WITH GARLIC AND ROSEMARY

8 oz. buffalo mozzarella cheese, chopped

2 garlic cloves, sliced

2 sprigs of rosemary

sea salt and freshly ground black pepper

PIZZA DOUGH

1⅔ cups all-purpose flour, plus extra for dusting

1 teaspoon active dry yeast (½ package)

1 teaspoon sea salt

1 tablespoon extra virgin olive oil, plus extra to serve

½–⅔ cup very warm water

a pizza stone or baking tray

Serves 2–4

To make the dough, sift the flour into the bowl of a food mixer fitted with a dough hook attachment, or a food processor fitted with a plastic blade. Add the yeast and salt, then work in the oil and water to form a soft dough.

Transfer the dough to a floured work surface. Knead for 5 minutes until the dough is smooth, roll into a ball, and put in an oiled bowl. Cover with plastic wrap and let rise in a warm place for about 45 minutes or until doubled in size.

Preheat the oven to its highest setting, about 500°F, and put a pizza stone or baking tray on the top shelf to heat.

Divide the risen dough in half and transfer one half to a well-floured surface. Roll it out to 12 inches in diameter. Take the hot stone or baking tray from the oven and carefully put the pizza base on top. Spread half the mozzarella, half the garlic, and half the rosemary leaves over the top, then season with salt and pepper, and sprinkle with a little oil. Bake in the preheated oven for 10 to 12 minutes until bubbling and lightly golden. Repeat with the second pizza.

It is best to eat the pizzas as soon as they come out of the oven, so share each one as they are cooked.

Not a pizza, not a tart, but halfway between the two, and totally delicious. Usually, a pizza is cooked on a preheated pizza stone so that the base will be crisp. You can use a preheated baking tray to achieve a good result.

MUSHROOM MASCARPONE PIZZAS

1 recipe Pizza Dough (page 81), or 2 packs pizza base mix (6½ oz. each), or 1 pack frozen pizza dough (16 oz.)

6 tablespoons extra virgin olive oil

2 garlic cloves, sliced

1 tablespoon chopped fresh thyme leaves

1 lb. small cremini mushrooms, sliced, about 5 cups

8 oz. mascarpone cheese

½ cup freshly grated Parmesan cheese

all-purpose flour, for dusting

sea salt and freshly ground black pepper

a pizza stone or baking tray

Serves 2–4

Make the pizza dough according to the directions on page 81 or, if using dried pizza dough mix, prepare the dough according to the directions on the package. If using frozen pizza dough, let it defrost and then proceed. Put the prepared dough in an oiled bowl, cover with plastic wrap, and let rise in a warm place for about 45 minutes or until doubled in size.

Preheat the oven to its highest setting, about 500°F, and put a pizza stone or baking tray on the top shelf to heat.

Heat the oil in a skillet and sauté the garlic and thyme for 1 minute. Add the mushrooms and sauté for another 4 to 5 minutes until they are brown but haven't started to release their juices. Season with salt and pepper.

Divide the risen dough in half and transfer one half to a well-floured surface. Roll it out to 12 inches in diameter. Remove the hot pizza stone or baking tray from the oven and carefully put the pizza base on top. Spoon half the mushrooms on top and dot with half the mascarpone. Sprinkle with half the Parmesan and bake in the preheated oven for 10 to 12 minutes until bubbling and golden. Serve at once and then repeat to make a second pizza.

FONDUE

If you've got a fondue set hidden away somewhere,
bring it out and dust it off! If you don't have
one, buy one. It's one of the most fun ways of
entertaining you can imagine. And one of the
simplest. You need a cast-iron dish for cheese
fondues rather than one of those metal pots. Just
add some good-quality Swiss or Alpine French
cheese, a glass of crisp white wine, and some crusty
bread, and you're off. Here you will find some
funky fondues for the more adventurous such as
Blue Cheese Fondue with Walnut Grissini, and
Cheddar and Calvados Fondue, which is made
with cider. Santé!

The traditional Swiss fondue, from the canton of Neuchâtel, is made from Gruyère and Emmental cheeses. There are many slight variations of this classic recipe; some use arrowroot, potato starch, or cornstarch instead of all-purpose flour, sometimes this is combined with the cold wine first, or added later with the Kirsch.

NEUCHÂTEL FONDUE

1 garlic clove, cut in half

1¼ cups dry white wine, such as Neuchâtel or Sauvignon Blanc

13 oz. Gruyère cheese, coarsely grated, about 3–3½ cups

13 oz. Emmental cheese, coarsely grated, about 3–3½ cups

1 tablespoon all-purpose flour

2–4 tablespoons Kirsch

freshly ground black pepper

2½ lb. crusty bread, cut into cubes (about 3–4 cups per person), to serve

Serves 6

Rub the cut side of the garlic around the inside of the fondue pot. Pour in the wine and bring it to a boil on top of the stove. Reduce the heat to simmering.

Put the grated cheese in a bowl, add the flour, and toss well. Gradually add the cheese to the wine, stirring constantly, and letting each addition melt into the wine.

When the mixture is creamy and smooth, add Kirsch and pepper to taste, then transfer the pot to its tabletop burner. Arrange the bread on serving platters.

To eat, spear a piece of bread onto a fondue fork, then dip it into the cheese mixture, swirling the fork in a figure-of-eight to keep the fondue smooth.

VARIATIONS
Other Swiss cantons created their own variations, usually by substituting their local cheese and wine. Try it with your own local dry wines and Gruyère-style cheeses:
Fondue Fribourgeois Substitute 3½ cups Vacherin Fribourgeois or fontina cheese, rind removed, finely chopped, for either the Gruyère or Emmental.
Comté Fondue Comté is a big, rich, fruity, Gruyère-type cheese, suitable for fondues. Use 7 cups instead of the Gruyère and Emmental.

Blue cheese and fresh walnuts make a delicious combination. This fondue is perfect served as an appetizer with asparagus, or as a dessert with juicy pears.

BLUE CHEESE FONDUE WITH WALNUT GRISSINI

½ cup sweet white wine such as Gewürztraminer

14 oz. creamy blue cheese, such as Gorgonzola or Roquefort, coarsely chopped, about 3½ cups

1 teaspoon cornstarch mixed with 1 tablespoon of the wine

4–6 ripe pears, quartered, or 24 asparagus spears, lightly cooked, to serve

WALNUT GRISSINI

3 cups all-purpose flour, plus extra for dusting

1 package (¼ oz.) active dry yeast

¾ cup fresh shelled walnuts

1 teaspoon sea salt

2 tablespoons walnut oil

a baking tray

Serves 6

To make the walnut grissini, put the flour, yeast, walnuts, and salt in a food processor fitted with a plastic blade. With the machine running, add the oil and ¾ cup water through the feed tube. Blend in 15-second bursts until it forms a soft mass. Turn out onto a floured board and knead for 2 minutes. Put the dough in an oiled bowl, cover, and let rest for 1 hour.

Knead again lightly and flatten to a rectangle about 16 x 6 inches. Cut crosswise into ½-inch strips, roll and stretch out each strip to about 12 inches in length, and transfer to a baking tray (you will need to bake in two batches). Cook in a preheated oven at 400°F for 16 to 18 minutes. Remove from the oven and let cool on a wire rack. Serve immediately or store in an airtight container for up to 1 week.

To prepare the fondue, pour the wine into a small metal fondue pot and heat until simmering. Gradually stir in the blue cheese, then the cornstarch mixture, stirring constantly until smooth. Transfer the pot to its tabletop burner and serve with the walnut grissini and pears or asparagus.

Vacherin is one of the world's great cheeses. All three varieties are unpasteurized, so are difficult to find in America. Vacherin Fribourgeois, the one used in cooking and to make fondues, is a little less sweet than Emmental, and so is perfect with the sweetness of caramelized shallots. Fontina or raclette cheese are suitable alternatives.

VACHERIN FONDUE WITH CARAMELIZED SHALLOTS

2 tablespoons butter or olive oil

10 oz. shallots, thinly sliced (if unavailable, use minced mild onions)

2 teaspoons light brown sugar

2 tablespoons balsamic or cider vinegar

2 cups dry white wine

10 oz. Gruyère cheese, grated, about 2–2½ cups

1 tablespoon all-purpose flour

10 oz. fontina or raclette cheese, grated, about 2–2½ cups

2 tablespoons port (optional)

TO SERVE

bread, such as sourdough or baguette, cubed

cherry tomatoes

a selection of fresh vegetables

Serves 6

Put the butter or oil in a cheese fondue pot and melt over medium heat. Add the shallots, reduce the heat to low, and cook for 10 minutes. Add the sugar and vinegar, stir to mix, and cook for another 10 minutes. Remove a few shallots and set them aside for serving.

Pour in the wine, bring to a boil, then reduce to a simmer.

Put the Gruyère and flour in a bowl and toss well. Gradually add the cheese to the simmering fondue mixture, stirring constantly. Stir in the fontina or raclette, then the port, if using.

Transfer the fondue pot to its tabletop burner, add the reserved shallots, and serve the fondue with cubes of bread, cherry tomatoes, and a selection of vegetables for dipping. Alternatively, put slices of baguette into 6 individual bowls and ladle the fondue over the top.

Potato rösti (pancakes) are a favorite Swiss dish. This apple version here is the perfect foil for a Cheddar fondue, flavored with the fiery apple brandy, Calvados. Cheddar cheeses are traditionally served with apples, so it's an apt match.

¾ cup hard cider

13 oz. Cheddar cheese, coarsely grated, about 3–3½ cups

1 tablespoon all-purpose flour

¼ cup Calvados or apple brandy

freshly ground black pepper

crisp sautéed bacon, to serve (optional)

APPLE RÖSTI

1 lb. potatoes, about 3–4, peeled

10 oz. apples, about 2, peeled

freshly squeezed juice of 1 lemon

½ teaspoon sea salt

1 tablespoon olive oil

freshly ground black pepper

a nonstick skillet, 9 inches diameter

Serves 6

CHEDDAR AND CALVADOS FONDUE WITH APPLE RÖSTI

To make the rösti, grate the potatoes on the coarse side of a box grater. Put in a bowl, cover with water, and let soak for 10 minutes. Drain in a colander, then put on a clean, lintfree dishtowel, squeeze out very well, and transfer to a clean dry bowl. Grate the apples into the original bowl, add the lemon juice to stop discoloration, toss well, then squeeze out in the lintfree dishtowel. Put the apple with the potato, add the salt and pepper, and mix well.

Put half the oil in the skillet, heat well, add the potato mixture, press down with a fork, and reduce the heat to medium-low. Cook the rösti for 10 minutes until brown underneath, loosen with a spatula, then turn out onto a large plate. Wipe around the skillet, add the remaining oil and heat, then slide the rösti back into the skillet to brown the other side. Cook for another 10 minutes until cooked through. Keep warm in the oven until needed.

Pour the cider into a fondue pot and bring to a boil. Reduce the heat to a simmer. Put the grated cheese and flour in a bowl and toss with a fork. Gradually add the cheese to the pot, stirring constantly, letting each addition melt into the cider. When creamy and smooth, add the Calvados or brandy and pepper to taste.

To serve, slice the rösti into 12 wedges, put 2 of them onto each warmed plate, and top with crisp bacon, if using, and a ladle of the hot fondue.

ENTRÉES

Whether it's a cook-to-impress dinner party or a simple family lunch, cheese can play the same starring role as meat or fish. Use it as the base for a show-stopping main course like the Feta and Chickpea Bundles, Roasted Vegetable and Ricotta Loaf, or Three-Colored Rice and Cheese Cake, or enjoy an outdoor cook-up of Parmesan Patties, a sophisticated twist on the traditional burger. It goes without saying that these recipes are great for vegetarians, but non-vegetarians will hardly notice they're missing meat.

Perfectly set eggs spiked with the fragrance of mixed fresh herbs makes a perfect supper dish, and it tastes even better if you dot the frittata with a little ricotta just before the top is broiled. Cut into small squares, frittata makes great finger food, too.

FRITTATA WITH FRESH HERBS AND RICOTTA

6 eggs

a large handful of chopped mixed fresh herbs, such as basil, chervil, chives, marjoram, mint, and/or parsley

1 teaspoon celery salt (optional)

2 tablespoons extra virgin olive oil

4 oz. fresh ricotta cheese, about ½ cup, crumbled into big pieces

sea salt and freshly ground black pepper

a nonstick skillet

Serves 4

Put the eggs in a bowl, add the herbs, celery salt, if using, and a good sprinkling of salt and pepper. Beat with a fork.

Preheat the broiler. Over the stove, heat the oil in a nonstick skillet until hot, then add the egg mixture. Cook over medium heat for 5 to 6 minutes until almost set. Dot the ricotta over the top, then cook under a hot broiler until the surface is set and browned.

Let cool slightly, then cut in wedges, and serve warm.

This looks splendid displayed whole before being sliced. The cross-section looks good, too—a vision of colorful vegetables interwoven with creamy ricotta. It keeps well in the refrigerator for a couple of days.

ROASTED VEGETABLE AND RICOTTA LOAF

2 eggplants, cut lengthwise into about 5 slices

olive oil, for brushing

1 red bell pepper, cut in half and seeded

1 yellow bell pepper, cut in half and seeded

2 zucchini, sliced lengthwise

8 oz. ricotta cheese, about 1 cup

2 tablespoons freshly squeezed lemon juice

1 garlic clove, crushed

a large handful of flat-leaf parsley, finely chopped

1 red chile, such as serrano, seeded and finely chopped

1 tablespoon balsamic vinegar

a large handful of basil leaves, torn

sea salt and freshly ground black pepper

2 large baking trays

a 2-lb. loaf pan

Serves 6–8

Preheat the oven to 400°F. Put the slices of eggplant on a baking tray, brush with olive oil, and sprinkle with salt and pepper. On another baking tray, put the red and yellow bell peppers and the zucchini, and sprinkle with salt. Put both trays in the preheated oven, with the eggplant in the hottest part of the oven. Roast until the peppers begin to blister and the zucchini are tender, about 20 minutes, and until the eggplant is tender, 20 to 25 minutes.

While the vegetables are roasting, put the ricotta in a bowl, add the lemon juice, garlic, parsley, chile, salt, and pepper, and mix.

When the eggplant is cooked, sprinkle with the vinegar. Put a damp cloth over the bell peppers and set aside for 5 to 10 minutes (this makes the skins steam off and you can peel them more easily). Peel the peppers and cut each piece in half again.

Line the loaf pan with plastic wrap, then gently press slices of eggplant over the bottom and sides of the pan. Reserve 4 slices for the top. Spread generously with some of the ricotta mixture, then add a layer of yellow bell pepper, taking it up the sides of the pan if you can. Sprinkle with some of the basil, then spread with more ricotta mixture. Layer the red bell pepper next, followed by zucchini, adding a layer of the ricotta and basil after each vegetable. Top with the reserved eggplant slices. Cover the top with plastic wrap, and put a weight on top. Leave overnight in the refrigerator.

Invert the loaf onto a plate and carefully pull away the plastic wrap. Using a serrated knife, cut into thick slices, and serve.

5 tablespoons unsalted butter

1 tablespoon olive oil

1 garlic clove, crushed

4 cups vegetable broth

1 cup polenta or yellow cornmeal

8 scallions, thinly sliced

4 oz. spinach, thinly sliced,
about 2–3 cups

8 oz. mozzarella cheese, sliced

¼ cup balsamic vinegar

sea salt and freshly ground
black pepper

ROASTED VEGETABLES

1½ lb. butternut squash, peeled, cut
in half, with seeds removed

1 red Cubanelle pepper, cut in half
and seeded, or regular bell pepper

1 yellow Cubanelle pepper, cut in half
and seeded, or regular bell pepper

2 red onions, cut into wedges

1 whole head of garlic, cloves
separated but skins left on

4 heads of baby fennel, quartered,
or 2 medium heads of fennel,
thickly sliced

a handful of thyme sprigs, with stalks

a handful of oregano sprigs, with stalks

2 sprigs of fresh rosemary

¼ cup olive oil

8 oz. cherry tomatoes

15 asparagus spears

2 large baking trays, 14 x 9 inches

a cookie cutter, 3 inches diameter

Serves 4

Roasting must be one of the simplest of all cooking techniques. It reinforces the idea that when good-quality ingredients are used, very little has to be done to them. In this recipe, roasting brings out the natural sweetness of the vegetables, which is complemented by the contrasting oaky flavor of balsamic vinegar.

SPINACH AND MOZZARELLA POLENTA
with roasted vegetables, herbs, and balsamic

To make the polenta, put the butter, oil, and garlic in a medium saucepan. Cook lightly, then add the broth and bring to a boil. Pour in the polenta, beating constantly, then add the scallions and spinach. Add salt and pepper to taste, then continue stirring. Cook for about 15 minutes or as instructed on the polenta package—the time will vary depending on the type of polenta used. Spoon into one of the baking trays and set aside for about 2 hours, or until firm to the touch.

To roast the vegetables, put all the vegetables, except the tomatoes and asparagus, on the second baking tray. Sprinkle with the herbs, olive oil, salt, and pepper, and mix well. Roast in a preheated oven at 400°F for 30 minutes, then stir in the tomatoes and asparagus. Continue cooking for another 20 minutes until all the vegetables are tender.

Invert the polenta onto the counter and cut out 8 discs with the cookie cutter. Brush the baking tray with olive oil and arrange the discs on it. Top each disc with a slice of mozzarella and bake in the oven for 10 to 15 minutes.

Put 2 discs of polenta on each plate, add the roasted vegetables, then sprinkle with 1 tablespoon balsamic vinegar. Serve immediately.

These layers of sweet orange squash and molten cheese provide a truly stunning focal point to any meal. Try them with slow-cooked red cabbage, juniper, and chile, plus potato mashed with scallions on the side. A mixed green salad could be substituted for the mashed potatoes, since the butternut squash and goat cheese is deceptively filling. For meat-eaters, this dish goes well with roast pork.

BUTTERNUT SQUASH AND GOAT CHEESE LAYERS

2 butternut squash

4 oz. fresh goat cheese, crumbled, about 1 cup

1 cup fresh bread crumbs

¼ cup thick, whole-milk yogurt

1 tablespoon fresh marjoram leaves

1 tablespoon fresh thyme leaves

olive oil, for sprinkling

sea salt and freshly ground black pepper

paprika, to serve

a baking tray, lightly greased

Serves 4, makes about 8 stacks

Cut the long, seedless section of squash into 1-inch slices. Reserve the bulbous part of the squash for another use. Peel the slices, then cook them in boiling salted water for 10 minutes, or until tender. Drain.

Put the goat cheese, bread crumbs, yogurt, herbs, salt, and pepper in a bowl and mix.

Put 4 slices of squash on the baking tray, top with some of the cheese mixture, then with another slice of squash. Repeat until you have used up all the squash and cheese.

Sprinkle the top of each stack with olive oil and bake in a preheated oven at 400°F for 30 minutes. Serve 2 stacks each, sprinkled with a little paprika.

Ideal for an indulgent lunch or supper dish, this creamy rice cake oozes with mozzarella, and has pockets of tomatoes bursting with flavor. You could even add a layer of cubed mozzarella to the middle of the tart, so that the center exudes strings of melted cheese when you cut it.

THREE-COLORED RICE AND CHEESE CAKE

¼ cup cornmeal or dried bread crumbs

about 6 cups fresh or 8 oz. frozen whole leaf spinach, thawed

3 eggs, beaten

2 cups plus 2 tablespoons arborio risotto rice (not long-grain)

1 tablespoon olive oil

2 tablespoons butter

1 onion, finely chopped

freshly grated nutmeg

8 oz. tiny cherry tomatoes, about 1½ cups

6 oz. mozzarella cheese, drained and cubed, about 1½–2 cups

¼ cup freshly grated Parmesan cheese

sea salt and freshly ground black pepper

a nonstick springform cake pan, 8 inches diameter, well buttered

Serves 6

Dust the prepared cake pan with the cornmeal or dried bread crumbs.

If using fresh spinach, tear off the stems. Wash the leaves well, then put them, still wet, in a covered saucepan and cook over medium heat for a few minutes until wilted. Drain well but do not squeeze dry—you want large pieces of spinach. If using thawed spinach, lightly squeeze it to remove excess moisture and toss the leaves a little to loosen them. Mix the spinach into the beaten eggs.

Cook the rice in a large saucepan of boiling salted water for 10 minutes, until almost tender, then drain through a strainer and tip into a large bowl. Meanwhile, heat the oil and butter in a skillet. Add the onion and cook until golden. Stir into the rice.

Season the egg and spinach mixture with nutmeg, salt, and pepper. Stir into the rice, then fold in the cherry tomatoes, mozzarella cubes, and Parmesan. Spoon into the prepared cake pan and level the surface.

Bake in a preheated oven at 400°F for 25 to 30 minutes, until firm and golden. Invert onto a plate, cut into wedges, and serve hot.

These patties make great outdoor food. Kids and grown-ups can't resist burgers and these are no exception. Make them in advance to save time, then chill or freeze until needed. Oven-bake rather than grill outdoors for best results.

1 tablespoon olive oil, plus extra for brushing

2 onions, chopped

4 oz. mushrooms, coarsely chopped, about 1 cup

1 teaspoon fresh thyme leaves

½ cup coarsely grated Parmesan cheese

½ cup grated Cheddar cheese

1 cup canned cranberry or pinto beans, rinsed and drained

1 cup fresh bread crumbs

1 tablespoon soy sauce

2 tablespoons red wine

1 teaspoon Dijon mustard

1 egg, beaten

1 tablespoon cornstarch

8 soft bread rolls

sea salt and freshly ground black pepper

TO SERVE (OPTIONAL)

salad greens or arugula

sliced tomatoes

sliced red onions

tomato ketchup

mayonnaise

chile sauce

a baking tray, lightly greased

Makes about 8 patties

PARMESAN PATTIES

Heat the oil in a skillet, add the onions, mushrooms, thyme, and salt, and sauté until the onions are softened and golden. Let cool.

Transfer the onion mixture to a food processor, add the Parmesan, Cheddar, beans, bread crumbs, and ground black pepper. Pulse until mixed, then add the soy sauce, wine, mustard, egg, and cornstarch. Blend until mixed, but not too smooth.

Using wet hands, shape the mixture into 8 balls, then flatten into 1-inch thick patties. Put on the prepared baking tray, cover with plastic wrap, and chill until firm. (At this point, you can freeze the patties, then cook from frozen when needed.)

When ready to cook, preheat the oven to 425°F. Remove the plastic wrap and brush the tops of the patties with extra oil. Bake in the preheated oven for 25 minutes until golden and crisp (5 to 10 minutes longer if cooking from frozen).

Cut the rolls in half and toast, grill, or broil lightly on one side, add the baked patties and your choice of accompaniments, then serve.

8 oz. phyllo pastry dough
(½ package)

2½ tablespoons butter, melted

FILLING FOR THE BUNDLES

10 oz. tomatoes (about 3 small)

1 tablespoon olive oil

1 teaspoon coriander seeds

1 teaspoon cumin seeds

1 garlic clove, crushed

½ red chile, seeded and finely chopped

1 cup couscous

⅓ cup dried chickpeas, soaked in
water overnight, drained, and cooked
for 1–1½ hours

3 oz. dried apricots, about ½ cup,
soaked in water overnight,
drained, and sliced

⅓ cup raisins, soaked in
water overnight

¾ cup slivered almonds, lightly
toasted in a dry skillet

a handful of flat-leaf parsley,
finely chopped

a handful of fresh mint leaves,
finely chopped

7 oz. feta cheese, cubed, about 2 cups

freshly squeezed juice of 1 lemon

sea salt and freshly ground
black pepper

RED ONION, TOMATO, AND OLIVE CHUTNEY

1 lb. tomatoes (about 4 small)

1 red onion, finely chopped

1 tablespoon olive oil

½ cup pitted black olives, finely chopped

2 baking trays

Serves 4

These pastries are delicious eaten cold, or serve them hot with spinach wilted with a pinch of nutmeg and grated lemon zest. A bowl of yogurt spiced with toasted chile, turmeric, coriander, and cumin makes a great accompaniment.

FETA AND CHICKPEA BUNDLES

with onion and tomato chutney

To make the filling for the bundles, put the tomatoes in a bowl, add the olive oil, spices, garlic, and chile, and mix. Season with salt, then tip onto a baking tray. Roast in a preheated oven at 400°F for 20 minutes until the tomatoes collapse in on themselves.

To prepare the chutney, cut the tomatoes into quarters and put them on a baking tray. Add the red onion and sprinkle with olive oil, then roast at 400°F for 20 minutes until tender. Transfer to a bowl, add the olives, and mix thoroughly. Add salt and pepper to taste.

Meanwhile, put the couscous in a bowl, add 1¾ cups cold water, and let soak for 10 minutes. Fluff up with a fork, then transfer to a large bowl with the soaked chickpeas, apricots, raisins, almonds, herbs, feta, lemon juice, salt, and pepper. Stir in the roasted whole tomatoes and mix well.

Reduce the oven to 350°F. Put 3 sheets of the phyllo dough on a counter, overlaying them so that they form a star shape, and brushing each sheet lightly with the melted butter before adding the next. (Keep the rest of the phyllo covered with a damp cloth.) Divide the filling into 4 portions and put 1 portion in the middle of the top sheet of phyllo, then pull up all the sides, twisting and pinching so that the filling is encased and the dough is sealed. Repeat to make 4 bundles. Bake for 20 minutes until lightly golden, then cover with foil and cook for a further 15 minutes.

Serve the bundles with the chutney on the side, and perhaps some wilted lemon spinach and spicy yogurt (see recipe introduction).

Roquefort has a particularly creamy yet salty and piquant flavor, but you could substitute any good-quality blue cheese when making this recipe.

8 oz. cream cheese, about 1 cup

⅔ cup heavy cream or crème fraîche

3 large eggs, beaten

7 oz. Roquefort or other good blue cheese (a scant 1 cup)

freshly grated nutmeg

3 tablespoons chopped fresh chives

freshly ground black pepper

DOUGH

2 cups all-purpose flour, plus extra for dusting

1 teaspoon salt

1 stick plus 1 tablespoon unsalted butter, softened

1 extra-large egg yolk

2½–3 tablespoons ice water

WALNUT AND TOASTED GARLIC DRESSING

2 tablespoons olive oil

3 garlic cloves, very thinly sliced

3 oz. walnut halves (about 1 cup)

1 tablespoon walnut oil

3 tablespoons chopped fresh parsley

a removable-bottomed tart pan, 10 inches diameter

foil or parchment paper and baking beans

Serves 6

ROQUEFORT TART
with walnut and toasted garlic dressing

To make the dough, sift the flour and salt together onto a sheet of wax paper. Put the butter and egg yolk in a food processor and blend until smooth, then add the water and blend again. Add the flour and salt and pulse until just mixed. Transfer to a lightly floured counter and knead gently until smooth. Form into a ball, flatten slightly, and wrap in plastic wrap. Chill in the refrigerator for at least 30 minutes.

Let the dough return to room temperature. Roll it out thinly on a lightly floured counter, then line the tart pan with it. Prick the bottom all over, then chill or freeze for 15 minutes. Line the pie shell with foil or parchment paper, then fill with baking beans. Set on a baking tray and bake "blind" in the center of a preheated oven at 400°F for 10 to 12 minutes. Remove the foil or parchment paper and baking beans, and return the pie crust to the oven for 5 to 7 minutes longer to dry out completely.

To make the filling, put the cream cheese in a bowl and beat until softened. Beat in the cream and the eggs. Crumble in the blue cheese and mix gently. Season with lots of black pepper and nutmeg. Stir in the chives, and set aside.

Let the pie crust cool slightly and lower the oven temperature to 375°F. Pour the filling into the crust and bake for 30 to 35 minutes or until puffed and golden brown.

Meanwhile, to make the walnut and garlic dressing, heat the olive oil in a skillet and add the garlic and walnuts. Stir-fry until the garlic is golden and the walnuts browned. Stir in the walnut oil and parsley. Serve the tart warm or at room temperature with the warm dressing.

BREAD, BISCUITS, & CHUTNEY

Bread and cheese is one of those all-time great partnerships, like strawberries and cream or eggs and bacon. And it's worth going the extra mile to make it the best you can, ideally by baking your own. Once you get into the swing of kneading and pummeling, you'll discover it's easier than you might think, not to say therapeutic, as you'll find if you try the Pain de Campagne or delicious Raisin and Rosemary Bread. Homemade biscuits also make a great accompaniment to a cheeseboard. Give old-fashioned cream crackers a makeover by adding garlic and poppyseeds, or give them a flavorful twist of your own.

PERFECT PARTNERS

There's really nothing like a good hunk of Cheddar and a freshly baked loaf of bread—true food of the gods.

BREAD

Bread is a wonderful counterfoil to a fine cheese. Good all-purpose varieties include sourdough and other rough country breads, crusty whites, ciabatta, and flatbreads. What you need is some texture to set against the smoothness and richness of the cheese. Breads that generally work less well are soft milk breads and other sweet breads, and those that are already flavored with cheese—too much of a good thing. Some breads seem tailor-made for certain cheeses (see right).

SHOULD YOU SERVE BUTTER?

It's a question of taste and the type of cheese. With hard British cheeses like Cheddar, a good unsalted farmhouse butter is often quite welcome, though it really isn't necessary with a soft creamy cheese like Explorateur. No one's telling you you can't though.

DELICIOUS DUOS

- Baguette and Brie.
- Walnut bread with blue cheese.
- Olive bread with goat cheese or feta.
- Irish soda bread with Durrus.
- Pumpernickel bread with Cheddar.
- Light rye with Emmental.

BISCUITS

More controversial are biscuits. Some experts say they detract from
the cheese, but personally I like them, providing they're not too sweet.
Crackers and water-biscuits are probably the most flexible, and oatcakes
work well with English regional cheeses and the creamy oatmeal-coated
Scottish cheese, Caboc. Flavored biscuits can be quite effective—for
color as well as taste. Caraway and fennel seeds balance the pungency
of strong cheeses such as Munster, while biscuits flavored with herbs
have an affinity with lighter creamier cheeses like young goat cheese.
Charcoal biscuits can look fabulous with a snowy white cheese.

PAIN DE CAMPAGNE

3 cups all-purpose flour

¼ cup fine whole-wheat pastry flour

1½ teaspoons sea salt

about 1⅓ cups tepid water, preferably spring water (or use tap water that has been filtered, boiled, and cooled)

SOURDOUGH STARTER

about 3 cups all-purpose flour

½ cup tepid water, preferably spring water (or use tap water that has been filtered, boiled, and cooled), plus extra for feeding the starter

a baking tray or pizza stone

Makes 1 large loaf

To make the sourdough starter, put ¾ cup flour and the water in a small bowl and mix to a thick sticky paste. Cover the bowl with a damp cheesecloth and secure with an elastic band. Leave it in a draft free spot, re dampening the cloth as necessary

After 2 to 4 days the paste should have a skin and look bubbly. (It should have a milky scent. If it smells bad rather than slightly sour, or if there are no signs of life, throw it away and start again.) At this stage, give the starter its first feed. Add ¾ cup flour and enough tepid water to make a soft, sticky paste-like dough. Work the dough with a wooden spoon to get plenty of air into the mixture. Cover the bowl again with a damp cloth and leave, as before, for 24 hours.

The starter should look very active now. Stir well then remove and discard half of it. Add another ¾ cup flour and enough tepid water to make a dough as before. Cover and leave as before for 12 hours.

The sourdough starter should now look very active and ready to use. Add about ¾ cup flour and enough water to make a soft sticky dough. The dough should be bubbly again and ready to use after 6 to 8 hours.

To make the bread, mix the flours and salt in a large bowl. Make a well in the center, spoon 1 cup of the starter into it, and pour in the water. Mix to make a soupy batter, then gradually work in the flour to make a slightly soft dough. Depending on the consistency, you may need to add a little extra flour or water, 1 tablespoon at a time. Turn out the dough onto a lightly floured counter and knead thoroughly for 10 minutes until very smooth and elastic. Return the dough to the bowl, cover with plastic wrap, and let rise in a warm place until doubled in size, 2 to 6 hours.

Turn out the risen dough and punch down. Shape into a rough ball and dust with flour. Set the dough in a colander lined with a floured linen cloth. Slide the colander into a large plastic bag and inflate slightly. Let rise in a warm place until doubled in size, 2 to 4 hours.

Preheat the oven to 450°F. Put the baking tray or pizza stone in the oven to heat. Uncover the loaf and turn out onto the hot tray or stone. Bake until the loaf turns a dark golden brown and sounds hollow when tapped underneath, 30 to 35 minutes. Let cool on a wire rack.

A quick, simple bread that's perfect for cheese. This bread goes well with all kinds of cheeses especially young goat's milk cheeses, Cheddar-style cheeses, and creamy blues.

RAISIN AND ROSEMARY BREAD

1¼ cups white bread flour, plus extra for dusting

1 cup whole-wheat bread flour

¾ cup rye flour

1½ teaspoons fast-action yeast

1½ teaspoons fine sea salt

1 tablespoon finely chopped fresh rosemary leaves, plus 2 extra sprigs for topping

1 tablespoon soft brown sugar

1½ cups water (tepid if you're making it by hand, cold if you're using a bread machine)

2 tablespoons olive oil

½ cup raisins

a baking tray, lightly oiled

Makes 1 medium loaf

To make this in a bread machine:

Add the liquid and dry ingredients in the order recommended in your machine's manual, omitting the raisins.

Set to knead on the dough program, adding the raisins at the beep. Shape and cook.

Put the white, whole-wheat, and rye flours in a large bowl and mix. Add the yeast, sea salt, and rosemary, and stir. Dissolve the sugar in 2 tablespoons of the water. Make a well in the flour and pour in the dissolved sugar and olive oil, followed by the rest of the water. Start working the flour into the liquid with a wooden spoon, then mix with your hands until all the flour is incorporated.

Turn the dough out onto a lightly floured board or counter and knead for 5 minutes or until the dough begins to feel elastic. Flatten the dough and add half the raisins. Fold over and knead for a couple of seconds, then repeat with the remaining raisins. Carry on kneading for another 5 minutes until smooth. Put the dough in a large bowl, cover with a lightly dampened dishtowel, and leave for 45 to 50 minutes until doubled in size.

Tip the dough out of the bowl and punch it down to knock out the air. Roll up the dough into a long sausage shape, tucking in the ends. Put it on the prepared baking tray, make 3 or 4 diagonal cuts in the dough with a sharp knife, cover with the damp dishtowel, and leave for another 25 minutes.

Brush the top of the loaf lightly with water and scatter the remaining rosemary leaves on top, pressing them lightly into the dough. Bake in a preheated oven at 400°F for 35 to 40 minutes until the loaf is well browned and sounds hollow when you tap it on the bottom.

Let the loaf cool on a wire rack for at least 45 minutes before serving.

There's absolutely no point in baking biscuits yourself if nobody knows they're homemade, and the distinctive shape of these very easy crackers makes it clear they're not store-bought. They're versatile enough to accompany most cheeses.

GARLIC AND POPPYSEED CREAM CRACKERS

1¼ cups all-purpose flour, plus extra for dusting

1 teaspoon baking powder

½ teaspoon fine sea salt

1 teaspoon poppyseeds

4 tablespoons (½ stick) unsalted butter, chilled and cut into small pieces

⅓ cup light cream

½ teaspoon crushed garlic

2 baking trays, lightly greased

Makes 14–18 large crackers

Sift the flour, baking powder, and salt into a large bowl and add the poppyseeds. Rub the butter into the flour using the tips of your fingers until the mixture resembles bread crumbs. Mix the cream with the garlic and stir into the flour. Gradually add 3 tablespoons water, pulling the mixture together until it forms a ball. (The dough can also be made in a food processor.)

Turn the dough out onto a lightly floured board or counter and shape it into a smooth flat disc. Cut it in half and roll out each half thinly and evenly. Using a sharp knife, cut the dough into long triangles, about 6 inches long. Use a spatula to transfer them carefully to a baking tray, then prick them all over with a fork. Repeat with the remaining dough. Roll any trimmings together and re-roll to make a final batch of crackers.

Bake in a preheated oven at 375°F for about 15 minutes or until lightly browned. Transfer to a wire rack to cool.

VARIATIONS
Cumin and turmeric crackers Sift ½ teaspoon turmeric with the flour. Replace the poppyseeds with 1 teaspoon cumin seeds and omit the garlic. Good served with soft goat's and sheep's milk cheeses.

Fennel crackers Replace ¾ cup of the flour with whole-wheat flour. Omit the garlic and replace the poppyseeds with 1½ teaspoons fennel seeds. Delicious with washed rind cheeses such as French Munster and Reblochon.

Paprika and chile crackers Sift ½ teaspoon paprika with the flour. Replace the poppyseeds with several turns of a chile-based spice grind. Best served with rich creamy cheeses.

There are many varieties of pumpkin and this recipe can be used to preserve all of them. Make sure that the flesh is firm and not stringy, or it will spoil the finished texture of the chutney. By cutting the pumpkin by hand into ½-inch cubes, it retains its color and texture. However, if you are making large quantities, you may prefer to chop the vegetables in a food processor. It is great served with bread and cheese, but it also goes well with scrambled eggs or cold cuts.

PUMPKIN AND RED TOMATO CHUTNEY

1 lb. peeled and seeded firm pumpkin or butternut squash flesh, cut into ½-inch cubes, about 2 cups

1 large ripe tomato, peeled, seeded, and chopped, about 1 cup

1 large onion, chopped, about 1 cup

⅔ cup golden raisins

1¼ cups soft brown sugar

1 teaspoon salt

1 inch fresh ginger, peeled and finely chopped

1 garlic clove, finely chopped

a little freshly grated nutmeg

1 cup malt vinegar, plus ½ cup extra (if unavailable; use apple cider vinegar)

1 sterilized canning jar, 1 pint, with screw band and new lid*

Makes 1 pint

*To sterilize the jar, wash it in hot, soapy water, then rinse with scalding water. Put the jar on the counter on a clean dishtowel and fill with boiling water. Leave filled until ready to use.

Put the pumpkin, tomato, onion, golden raisins, sugar, salt, ginger, garlic, nutmeg, and the 1 cup vinegar in a large saucepan and bring slowly to a boil. Simmer for 1 hour, stirring from time to time. The chutney should look dark, dense, and rich. Add extra vinegar if it dries out too much while cooking.

Transfer the chutney to the hot jar, leaving ½ inch headspace. Wipe the rim clean with a damp paper towel and cap the jar. For a lasting seal, the jar should be processed in a boiling-water canner.

If you have a canner, put the rack in the bottom, set the jar in the rack, and add water to cover the top of the jar by 2 inches. Cover the canner. If you don't have a canner, you can improvise with a large stockpot, a lid, a heatproof plate, and clean dishtowels. Put a folded dishtowel in the bottom of the stockpot. Set the filled jar on top and put more folded towels around the jar to prevent it from hitting the sides while the water is boiling. Lay another towel on top and weight it down with a heatproof plate. Fill the pot with water to cover the top of the jar by 2 inches. Cover the pot.

Bring the water in the canner or stockpot slowly to a boil, and boil for 10 minutes. Remove the jar and let cool. Label, then store for 1 to 6 months in a cool, dark place before opening.

DESSERTS

Rich creamy cheeses such as mascarpone lend themselves perfectly to seductive sweet treats that will have your friends begging for the recipe. From Warm Chocolate Mascarpone Cheesecake to Mascarpone and Rose Fondue, this chapter is pure indulgence! Learn to use mascarpone as the base for an ultra-creamy ice cream to accompany Strawberries in Balsamic Vinegar or—a real treat for lovers of dark espresso coffee—as a sophisticated *semifreddo* frozen mousse. The cheese course will never be the same again …

SWEET HEAVEN ...
MASCARPONE AND RIPE PEACHES

SWEET CHEESE

Accompanied by fruits or drizzled with honey, soft creamy cheeses make a fabulous dessert.

DELICIOUS ...
CREAMY GORGONZOLA AND FRESH
FIGS DRIZZLED WITH HONEY

Cheeses that suit the sweet-toothed include fromage frais, Quark, and ultra creamy mascarpone (even if it doesn't strictly count as cheese). There's a fine dividing line between a cheese plate that serves as a savory and one that replaces a dessert, but if you're looking for the latter you don't want a cheese that's too salty, or fruit that's too tart. Summer combinations that work well include strawberries and fromage frais, cherries and cream cheese mixed with a little sour cream, and ripe peaches and mascarpone. In fall and winter you can serve fruit that has been poached or baked in a fruit syrup, such as pears or prunes in red wine, or a spiced fruit compote.

Drizzling a cheese with honey—even a blue cheese—immediately takes it into the dessert league, particularly if you accompany it with fruit—the classic combination being creamy Gorgonzola and fresh figs. Soft-set artisan jams, particularly those made from blueberries and plums, also taste good with rich creamy cheeses. And you can even bake an apple pie with cheese, as they do in Yorkshire, England, using the local Wensleydale cheese.

Mascarpone doubles for cream in all kinds of dishes including the famous Italian tiramisù (it's always a wicked combination with chocolate) and also makes luscious ice cream (see page 129). A particularly good dessert cheese is ricotta, which lends itself perfectly to baking and combines beautifully with lemon. It's a thrifty product made from the whey left over from making harder cheeses, and gives a lovely light creamy texture to Italian-style cakes and cheesecakes. Make sure you buy the sweet version and not the salty *ricotta salata*.

Strawberries with balsamic may sound strange, but this resinous syrup brings out their sweetness. Try a strawberry sorbet laced with a tablespoon of balsamic: undetectable, but it makes even the least flavorsome fruits taste better.

1½ lb. ripe strawberries, cut in half, about 5 cups

MASCARPONE ICE CREAM

2¼ cups whole milk

1 vanilla bean

5 large egg yolks

½ cup plus 2 tablespoons sugar

1⅓ cups heavy cream

1¼ cups mascarpone cheese

BALSAMIC SYRUP

1 cup sugar

2 tablespoons balsamic vinegar

an ice cream maker

Serves 4: makes 1 quart ice cream

STRAWBERRIES with balsamic syrup and mascarpone ice cream

To make the ice cream, put the milk in a saucepan. Split the vanilla bean lengthwise, scrape out the seeds, and add the bean and seeds to the milk. Heat until almost boiling, remove from the heat, stir well, and set aside to infuse for 30 minutes.

Put the egg yolks and sugar in a bowl and beat until pale and creamy. Add the milk and vanilla bean and mix well. Return the mixture to the pan and remove the vanilla bean (which can be rinsed, dried, and later used to flavor a jar of sugar). Cook the custard mixture over low heat, stirring constantly, until it is thick enough to coat the back of a wooden spoon. It must not boil or it will separate. Remove from the heat and stir in the cream. Let cool completely.

When cold, use a hand-held electric beater to beat the custard into the mascarpone. Chill, then freeze in an ice cream maker, transfer to a freezer container, and store in the freezer.

To make the balsamic syrup, put the sugar, balsamic vinegar, and 1 cup water in a small saucepan. Heat gently until the sugar dissolves. Bring to a boil and boil rapidly for 5 minutes until reduced by one-quarter. Remove from the heat, let cool, then chill.

Toss the strawberries in the syrup. Transfer the ice cream to the refrigerator at least 20 minutes before serving, to let it soften. Serve the strawberries with scoops of mascarpone ice cream, then trail any remaining syrup over the top.

A *semifreddo* is a dessert that is half frozen to give it a slightly thickened, creamy texture. Sometimes it is made of whipped cream lightened with meringue, then flavored with anything from vanilla to passionfruit. In this example, the espresso gives an interesting texture, but you must buy it very finely ground.

COFFEE SEMIFREDDO WITH ESPRESSO

1½ cups ricotta cheese, at room temperature

1½ cups mascarpone cheese, at room temperature

1 tablespoon dark rum

3 tablespoons Tia Maria, Kahlùa, or other coffee liqueur

1 teaspoon vanilla extract

¼ cup confectioners' sugar, or to taste

2 tablespoons finely ground espresso Italian roast coffee

TO SERVE

bittersweet chocolate wafers

6–8 tiny cups of hot espresso coffee

softly whipped cream (optional)

6–8 flexible ice cream molds or small ramekins

Serves 6–8

Put the ricotta and mascarpone in a bowl, and beat with a wooden spoon. (Do not attempt to do this in a food processor or the mixture will be too runny.) Beat in the rum, coffee liqueur, vanilla extract, and confectioners' sugar. Fold in the ground espresso so that the mixture is marbled. Carefully spoon into the ice cream molds or ramekins, piling the mixture high. Freeze for 2 hours.

Transfer to the refrigerator 15 to 20 minutes before serving to soften slightly. The mixture should be only just frozen or very chilled. Just before serving, dip the molds quickly in warm water and invert into chilled shallow bowls. Top with bittersweet chocolate wafers. Serve immediately with tiny cups of espresso for guests to pour over the *semifreddo* and some whipped cream, if using.

Rosewater is sold in Middle Eastern stores and supermarket baking sections. If unavailable use Amaretto liqueur or vanilla. If you toast and grind the almonds yourself, they will be fresher and have more texture.

MASCARPONE AND ROSE FONDUE
with almond syrup cookies

10 oz. mascarpone cheese, about 1¼ cups

¼ cup confectioners' sugar

2 tablespoons sweet Marsala wine or cream

½ teaspoon rosewater

ALMOND SYRUP COOKIES (OPTIONAL)

8 oz. blanched almonds, toasted, about 1½ cups

¾ cup sugar

finely grated zest and juice of 2 unwaxed lemons

1 egg

all-purpose flour, for dusting

TO SERVE

pomegranate seeds (optional)

sliced fruit, such as peaches, apricots, or nectarines

a baking tray, lined with baking parchment

Serves 6

To make the almond syrup cookies, if using, put the toasted almonds in a food processor and grind to a coarse mixture. Transfer to a bowl, then add ½ cup of the sugar and the lemon zest. Make a well in the center, add the egg, and mix well.

Transfer to a well-floured counter and shape into a flat log, 10 x 3 x ¾ inch deep. Cut into 20 to 24 slices. Place on the prepared baking tray, allowing room to spread, then bake in a preheated oven at 350°F for 18 minutes. Remove from the oven and transfer to a wire rack to cool.

Meanwhile, put the remaining ¼ cup sugar and the lemon juice in a saucepan and bring to a boil. Simmer for 3 minutes until syrupy. Let cool, then drizzle the mixture over the cookies.

Put the mascarpone, confectioners' sugar, and Marsala or cream in the top of a double boiler set over simmering water and heat, stirring until smooth. Stir in the rosewater. Transfer the mixture to a fondue pot set over its tabletop burner to keep warm. Scatter some pomegranate seeds over the fondue, if using.

Serve with the almond syrup cookies or other cookies and fruit slices for dipping.

This cheesecake is delicious and easy to make, too. Blending the sugar with lemon zest transfers the essential oils to the sugar and gives a wonderful aroma to the tart. Use cottage cheese instead of cream cheese to give a lighter texture.

SIMPLE LEMON CHEESECAKE

1⅔ cups all-purpose flour, plus extra for dusting

2 tablespoons confectioners' sugar

½ teaspoon salt

1 stick unsalted butter, chilled and cut into small pieces

2 egg yolks

2–3 tablespoons cold water

FILLING

grated zest and juice of 1 unwaxed lemon

⅓ cup sugar

1½ packages cream cheese, 8 oz. each, about 1½ cups

1 large egg, plus 3 egg yolks

2 teaspoons vanilla extract

a removable-bottomed tart pan, 9 inches diameter

parchment paper and ceramic baking beans or rice, or crumpled foil

Serves 4–6

To make the dough, sift the flour, confectioner's sugar, and salt into a large bowl. Add the butter and, using your fingertips, rub it in until the mixture resembles fine bread crumbs. Stir in the egg yolks mixed with at least 2 tablespoons cold water to make a firm but malleable dough. Transfer the dough to a lightly floured counter and knead until smooth. Shape the dough into a flattened ball, wrap in plastic wrap, and chill for at least 30 minutes.

Remove the dough from the refrigerator and let it return to room temperature. Roll it out on a lightly floured counter and line the tart pan with it. Prick the bottom all over with a fork, then chill or freeze for 15 minutes. Line the crust with parchment paper, then fill with baking beans or rice. Alternatively, line the cheesecake crust with crumpled foil. Set the tart pan on a baking tray and bake "blind" in the center of a preheated oven at 375°F for 10 minutes. Remove the parchment paper and baking beans or foil, and return the crust to the oven for another 10 minutes. Set the crust aside to cool; leave the oven on.

To make the filling, put the lemon zest and sugar in a food processor or blender and blend until the mixture looks damp. Add the lemon juice and blend again—the lemon zest should have completely dissolved in the sugar—then add the cream cheese, the whole egg, egg yolks, and vanilla extract, and blend until smooth. Pour the mixture into the cheesecake crust.

Bake the cheesecake in the preheated oven for 25 minutes or until just set and lightly browned on top. Remove from the oven and let cool. Serve at room temperature.

Blueberry cheesecake is a welcome way to round off any meal and this delicious version is a real crowd pleaser. You can substitute cranberries for blueberries at Thanksgiving or simply top with any fresh berries.

BLUEBERRY CHEESECAKE

15 graham crackers, about 3½ oz.

4 tablespoons unsalted butter, ½ stick

FIRST LAYER

16 oz. full-fat cream cheese, about 2 cups

2 large eggs

½ cup sugar

¼ teaspoon vanilla extract

SECOND LAYER

1¼ cups sour cream

⅔ cup thick, whole-milk yogurt

2½ tablespoons sugar

1 teaspoon vanilla extract

TOPPING

¼ cup superfine sugar

8 oz. blueberries, about 1½ cups

1 teaspoon arrowroot

a springform cake pan, 8 inches diameter

Serves 8–10

Put the graham crackers in a food processor and blend until crumbs form. Alternatively, put them in a plastic bag and crush with a rolling pin. Put the butter in a saucepan and melt gently. Let cool slightly, then stir in the crushed crackers. Press evenly into the bottom of the cake pan.

To make the first layer, put the soft cheese, eggs, sugar, and vanilla extract in a bowl and beat thoroughly. Pour it over the pie crust and smooth the top. Put the pan on a baking tray and bake in a preheated oven at 375°F for 20 minutes or until just set. Remove from the oven and set aside for 20 minutes to firm up. Leave the oven on.

To make the second layer, put the sour cream, yogurt, sugar, and vanilla extract in a bowl and mix. Spoon evenly over the first layer. Return the cheesecake to the preheated oven for 10 minutes, remove, and let cool. Once cool, refrigerate for at least 6 hours or overnight.

For the topping, put the sugar and 2 tablespoons water in a saucepan and heat gently until the sugar dissolves. Turn up the heat, add the blueberries, cover, and cook, shaking the pan occasionally, for about 5 minutes until the berries are soft. Remove from the heat. Mix the arrowroot with 2 tablespoons water and add to the blueberries. Stir over low heat until the juice has thickened. Set aside to cool, then check for sweetness, adding extra sugar to taste if necessary.

About an hour before serving ease a knife down the sides of the cake pan, then release the clamp and remove the sides. Spoon the blueberry topping evenly over the cheesecake and return to the refrigerator until ready to serve.

The truly tropical flavor of coconut, mango, and passionfruit are given a lift with coconut liqueur and orange and lime juice.

8 oz. graham crackers

4 tablespoons unsalted butter, ½ stick

¼ cup sugar

FILLING

1¼ cups canned coconut milk

1 vanilla bean

1 cup milk

4 large egg yolks

½ cup plus 2 tablespoons sugar

2 tablespoons powdered gelatin

⅔ cup mascarpone

3 tablespoons coconut liqueur

MANGO AND PASSIONFRUIT SAUCE

1 large ripe mango, about 1 lb., peeled and pit removed

freshly squeezed juice of 1 orange

freshly squeezed juice of 1 lime

2 ripe wrinkled passionfruit, cut in half and seeds reserved

confectioners' sugar, to taste

6 deep metal rings, 2½ inches diameter, about 2 inches deep, with a capacity of ½ cup, oiled (you can use washed and dried cans, opened at each end)

a baking tray

Serves 6

COCONUT CHEESECAKE
with mango and passionfruit sauce

Put the graham crackers in a food processor and blend until crumbs form. Alternatively, put them in a plastic bag and crush with a rolling pin. Put the butter and sugar in a small saucepan and melt gently. Let cool slightly, then stir in the crumbs. Stand the prepared rings on a baking tray and press a layer of the crumb mixture into the bottom of each one, then chill.

To make the filling, put the coconut milk in a non-aluminum saucepan and beat well. Split the vanilla bean lengthwise and scrape the black seeds into the coconut milk. Stir in the milk, heat to boiling point, then remove from the heat.

Put the egg yolks and sugar in a bowl and beat until pale and fluffy. Pour in the scalded coconut milk and stir well. Return to the pan and cook over gentle heat, stirring, until thickened like heavy cream, about 15 minutes. Do not boil, or it will curdle. Strain this custard into a bowl, cover with damp wax paper, and let cool. Put the gelatin and ¼ cup cold water in a small heatproof bowl and set aside for 5 minutes. Set the bowl over a saucepan of simmering water and let dissolve until clear. Stir occasionally, then let cool slightly. Put the mascarpone in a second bowl and beat in the liqueur to loosen it, then beat in the cooled custard. Stir the gelatin into the cheese mixture. Chill for 15 to 20 minutes until the custard starts to thicken slightly. Pour into the rings and chill for 2 to 3 hours until set.

To make the sauce, put the mango in a blender with the orange and lime juice, and blend until smooth. Press through a fine-mesh strainer into a bowl and stir in the passionfruit seeds. Add sugar to taste. If the sauce is a little too thick, add more orange juice. Chill.

To serve, loosen the cheesecakes, slide each one onto a plate, remove the rings, and spoon a little sauce over the top.

This rather unusual cheesecake from Italy can be eaten warm or at room temperature. The mascarpone gives it a slightly sweet taste and a rich texture.

8 oz. graham crackers or digestive biscuits

4 tablespoons unsalted butter, ½ stick

2 oz. bittersweet chocolate, finely chopped, about ½ cup

confectioners' sugar, for sprinkling

ice cream or thick cream, to serve

CHOCOLATE FILLING

2 extra large eggs, separated

a scant ½ cup sugar

8 oz. mascarpone cheese, about 1 cup

⅔ cup heavy cream, lightly whipped

½ cup very finely chopped dark chocolate

¼ cup unsweetened cocoa powder, sifted

1 cup slivered almonds, finely ground in a food processor, or ½ cup ground almonds

1–2 tablespoons Amaretto liqueur or brandy

a springform cake pan, 9 inches diameter, well buttered

Serves 8

WARM CHOCOLATE MASCARPONE CHEESECAKE

Put the crackers in a food processor and pulse until fine crumbs form. Alternatively, put them in a plastic bag and crush with a rolling pin. Transfer the crumbs to a large bowl. Put the butter and chocolate in the top of a double boiler set over steaming but not boiling water, and melt gently (do not let the bottom of the top pan touch the water). Remove from the heat, stir gently, then stir into the cracker crumbs. When well mixed, transfer the mixture to the prepared pan and, using the back of a spoon, press onto the bottom and about halfway up the sides of the pan. Chill.

To make the filling, put the egg yolks and sugar in a large bowl and, using an electric beater or mixer, beat until very thick and mousse-like—when the beaters are lifted, a wide ribbon-like trail slowly falls back into the bowl. Put the mascarpone in a separate bowl, beat until smooth, then gently fold in the whipped cream. Gently stir the mascarpone mixture into the egg yolks, then add the chopped chocolate, cocoa, ground almonds, and liqueur, and mix gently.

Put the egg whites in a spotlessly clean, greasefree bowl and beat with an electric beater until stiff peaks form. Using a large metal spoon, fold the egg whites into the mascarpone mixture in 3 batches.

Pour the filling into the pie crust and bake in a preheated oven at 325°F for about 1 hour or until set and beginning to color. Remove from the oven and let cool for about 20 minutes, then carefully unclip and remove the pan. Sprinkle with confectioners' sugar and serve warm or at room temperature with ice cream or thick cream.

INDEX

CONVERSION CHARTS

Weights and measures have been rounded up or down slightly to make measuring easier.

Volume equivalents:

American	Metric	Imperial
1 teaspoon	5 ml	
1 tablespoon	15 ml	
¼ cup	60 ml	2 fl.oz.
⅓ cup	75 ml	2½ fl.oz.
½ cup	125 ml	4 fl.oz.
⅔ cup	150 ml	5 fl.oz. (¼ pint)
¾ cup	175 ml	6 fl.oz.
1 cup	250 ml	8 fl.oz.

Oven temperatures:

110°C	(225°F)	Gas ¼
120°C	(250°F)	Gas ½
140°C	(275°F)	Gas 1
150°C	(300°F)	Gas 2
160°C	(325°F)	Gas 3
180°C	(350°F)	Gas 4
190°C	(375°F)	Gas 5
200°C	(400°F)	Gas 6
220°C	(425°F)	Gas 7
230°C	(450°F)	Gas 8
240°C	(475°F)	Gas 9

Weight equivalents:

Imperial	Metric
1 oz.	25 g
2 oz.	50 g
3 oz.	75 g
4 oz.	125 g
5 oz.	150 g
6 oz.	175 g
7 oz.	200 g
8 oz. (½ lb.)	250 g
9 oz.	275 g
10 oz.	300 g
11 oz.	325 g
12 oz.	375 g
13 oz.	400 g
14 oz.	425 g
15 oz.	475 g
16 oz. (1 lb.)	500 g
2 lb.	1 kg

Measurements:

Inches	Cm
¼ inch	5 mm
½ inch	1 cm
¾ inch	1.5 cm
1 inch	2.5 cm
2 inches	5 cm
3 inches	7 cm
4 inches	10 cm
5 inches	12 cm
6 inches	15 cm
7 inches	18 cm
8 inches	20 cm
9 inches	23 cm
10 inches	25 cm
11 inches	28 cm
12 inches	30 cm

CREDITS

PHOTOGRAPHY

Key: a=above, b=below, r=right, l=left, c=center

All photographs by DAVID MUNNS unless otherwise stated

WILLIAM LINGWOOD Pages 2–3, 30bl, 46, 48, 50–51, 67, 68–69, 72, 84–92, 94cl & bl, 98, 101, 102–103, 109, 124br, 133, endpapers

MARTIN BRIGDALE Pages 30ar, 34, 45, 52ac & br, 54, 61, 62, 64cl, 111, 112c, 116, 124al & cr, 134, 141

PETER CASSIDY Pages 29, 30al, 36, 42, 43, 52al, 64al & bl, 70, 80, 83, 94br, 96, 104

GUS FILGATE Pages 30cl, 32, 33, 38–39, 40–41

JEAN CAZALS Pages 124bl, 128, 131, 139

JASON LOWE Pages 64br, 74–78

TARA FISHER Pages 1, 112ar, 123

IAN WALLACE Pages 52bl, 56, 59

PHILIP WEBB Pages 37, 94ar, 106

RECIPES

FIONA BECKETT

Blueberry cheesecake
Garlic and poppyseed cream crackers
Raisin and rosemary bread

CELIA BROOKS BROWN is one of the talented teacher-chefs at the famous bookshop, Books For Cooks, in Notting Hill, London. Celia's books include the international bestseller *New Vegetarian* (Ryland Peters & Small).

Parmesan patties
Rarebit

MAXINE CLARK has taught in well-known cooking schools such as Leith's in London, and now teaches at Alastair Little's Tasting Places in Sicily and Tuscany. Her work appears regularly in magazines and newspapers. Her books include *Trattoria* and *Dolcissimo* (both Ryland Peters & Small).

Coconut cheesecake with mango and
   passionfruit sauce
Coffee semifreddo with espresso
Green lasagne with ricotta pesto and mushrooms
Parmesan chips
Mozzarella in carrozza
Pear, pecorino, and pea crostini
Prosciutto-wrapped bocconcini crostini
Roquefort tart with walnut and toasted
garlic dressing
Simple lemon cheese tart
Strawberries with balsamic and mascarpone
   ice cream
Three-colored rice and cheese cake

LINDA COLLISTER's books on baking have sold over 500,000 copies. Her bestselling books for Ryland Peters & Small include *Bread: from Sourdough to Rye* and *Chocolate*.

Pain de compagne
Warm chocolate mascarpone cheesecake

CLARE FERGUSON is a food writer with an international reputation. She has been the Food Editor of *Elle* and *She* magazines, and is the author of a number of books including *Mediterraneo* (Ryland Peters & Small).

Eggplant cheese fritters
Greek cheese savory

URSULA FERRIGNO is a talented cook, food writer and teacher, dividing her time between London and her homeland of Italy. She runs popular cookery courses in London and Tuscany.

Fontina and walnut risotto
Risotto with four cheeses
Risotto with watercress and Taleggio

SILVANO FRANCO'S work appears in magazines, including *Ideal Home*. She has presented her own cooking program on BBC TV—*The Best*.

Fusilli with salsa verde and char-grilled cheese
Pasta with prosciutto, arugula, and bubbling
   blue cheese
Three cheese baked penne

JANE NORAIKA is head chef at London's most celebrated vegetarian restaurant, Food for Thought. For Ryland Peters & Small she has written *New Vegetarian Entertaining*.

Butternut squash and goat cheese layers
Feta and chickpea bundles with onion and
   tomato chutney
Herb and feta polenta topped with sun-dried
   tomato tapenade
Roasted red bell pepper and goat cheese rolls
Roasted vegetable and ricotta loaf
Spinach and blue cheese phyllo pastries with
   apricots and pine nuts
Spinach and mozzarella polenta

LOUISE PICKFORD is a British food writer now living and working in Sydney. She contributes to several magazines including *Gourmet Traveller* and is the author of more than a dozen cookbooks, including *Grilling* (Ryland Peters & Small).

Baked chèvre
Cheese on toast
Frittata with fresh herbs and ricotta
Grilled pita salad with olive salsa
   and mozzarella
Mozzarella pizzas with garlic and
   rosemary
Mushroom mascarpone pizzas
Warm goat cheese soufflés
Zucchini, feta, and mint salad

FIONA SMITH is a food writer and food stylist from New Zealand, who also works in Europe. Her work appears in books, magazines,

advertising, and on television. She is the author of *Easy Sushi Rolls* (Ryland Peters & Small).

Blue cheese fondue with walnut grissini
Cheddar and calvados fondue with apple rösti
Mascarpone and rose fondue with almond syrup
   cookies
Neuchâtel fondue
Vacherin fondue with caramelized onions

LAURA WASHBURN trained at the prestigious Paris cooking school, Ecole de Cuisine La Varenne, and worked with Patricia Wells, author of *A Food Lover's Guide to Paris*. She has written *Kitchen Suppers* for Ryland Peters & Small.

Belgian endive salad with Roquefort and celery
Cauliflower gratin
Potatoes with Reblochon

LINDY WILDSMITH is well known from her appearances in the celebrity kitchen at *House & Garden* fairs. She has her own cooking school and works with famous chef Franco Taruschio, formerly of the legendary Walnut Tree restaurant, staging popular hands-on Italian lunch party cooking days.

Pumpkin and red tomato chutney